Disclaimer and Legal Notice. This product is not legal or medical advice and should not be interpreted in that manner. You need to do your own due diligence to determine if the content of this product is right for you. The author, publisher, distributors, and or/affiliates of this product are not liable for any damages or losses associated with the Content of this product. While every attempt has been made to verify the information shared in this publication, neither the author, publisher, distributors, and/or affiliates assume any responsibility for errors, omissions, or contrary interpretation of the subject matter herein. Any perceived slights to any specific person(s) or organization(s) are purely unintentional. We have no control over the nature, content, and availability of the websites listed in this book. The inclusion of any website links does not necessarily imply a recommendation or endorse the views expressed within them. DYM Worldwide Publishers take no responsibility for, and will not be liable for, the websites being temporary or being removed from the Internet. The accuracy and completeness of the information provided herein, and opinions stated herein are not guaranteed or warranted to produce any particular results, and the advice or strategies, contained herein may not be suitable for every individual. The author, publisher, distributors, and/or affiliates shall not be liable for any loss incurred as a consequence of the use and application, directly or indirectly of any information presented in this work. This publication is designed to provide information regarding the subject matter covered. The information included in this book has been compiled to give an overview of the topics covered. The information contained in this book has been compiled to provide an overview of the subject. It is not intended as medical advice and should not be construed as such. For a firm diagnosis of any medical conditions, you should consult a doctor or veterinarian (as related to animal health). The writer, publisher, distributors, and/or affiliates of this work are not responsible for any damages or negative consequences following any of the treatments or methods highlighted in this book. Website links are for informational purposes only and should not be seen as a personal endorsement; the same applies to any products or services mentioned in this work. The reader should also be aware that although the web links included were correct at the time of writing they may become out of date in the future. Any pricing or currency exchange rate information was accurate at the time of writing but may become out of date in the future. The Author, Publisher, distributors, and/or affiliates assume no responsibility for pricing and currency exchange rates mentioned within this work.

Table of Contents

Introduction

Do you have a checklist of the qualities that you are looking for in a dog? Maybe one of these qualities is being a low-maintenance dog that you don't need to bring to the pet groomer every week. Or, do you want a dog that can keep up with you as you trail tough terrains, and at the same time can rest on your lap and get cozy with you at home? If these are some qualities that you are looking for in a dog, then you definitely need to know more about the Vizsla.

The Vizsla is a well-built working dog with defined muscles that need ample space to run.

Vizslas are gaining popularity as the athletic and loyal breed of choice for aspiring dog owners.

If you are the type of person who leads an active outdoor lifestyle and wants a dog who can keep up with your pace while giving you its loving devotion, then you might want to consider choosing a Vizsla. The Vizsla is a well-built working dog with defined muscles that needs ample space to run. It is very energetic, and you would need to channel that energy by allowing it to exercise for at least 60 minutes per day.

This regal breed hailed from Hungary and was used by the nobles as pointer dogs when hunting. Their excellent sense of smell was highly prized as their owners hunted for fowl and upland game. This breed was intended to work in the field, water, or forest. You will be amazed when you see a Vizsla in its natural environment when it moves in powerful strides in different terrains, and as it exhibits its natural hunting instincts.

Vizslas are intelligent, gentle, and affectionate. They will not hold back in showering you with their affection. They are eager to please their owners while being fearless and protective. When they are not out running with you, they will be by your side or on your lap and enjoy your company. They are excellent companion dogs that would fit perfectly in your family.

This breed also requires low maintenance, thanks to its short coat that is easy to clean. They are also generally strong and healthy but are also susceptible to health issues like hip dysplasia, and eye disease.

This book will introduce you to the beautiful breed that is the Vizsla. It will help you explore its fascinating history and characteristics, and know what it needs to live happily with you. The information in this book will help you determine if this is the right dog for you and if you are the type of owner that a Vizsla needs. If you do choose the Vizsla, then this book can be your reference guide for your journey with your Vizsla, along the way.

CHAPTER 1

Where Did the Vizsla Come From?

The Vizsla has a regal history and background. The breed originated in Hungary and became a loyal companion to kings, warlords, and nobles. They have been around for almost a thousand years, and their ancestors go back as far as the 10th century. The breed was preserved and maintained for hundreds of years by the nobles. The dogs were held in high regard by their owners and were known as the "Gift of Kings" as they were chosen to be presented to foreign royalty.

The Vizsla has a regal history and background. The breed originated in Hungary and became a loyal companion to kings, warlords, and nobles.

Vizsla History and Background

The Vizsla is mentioned in the earliest times of Hungarian history. The Vizsla's ancestors were the trusted hunting dogs of the Magyar tribe, who served as their right-hand, during hunts. The Magyar tribe thrived in the Carpathian Basin in the Eighth Century; primitive stone etchings more than a thousand years old present the Magyar hunter, his falcon, and a dog- presumed to be Vizsla.

The 'Illustrated Vienna Chronicle' of 1357 holds the first written record of the Vizsla, which was known during this time as the Hungarian Pointer. In the 1600s, documents found in archives depicted people living in mansions, breeding Vizslas. This information concluded that Vizslas were bred to hunt small game.

Before the 18th century, wealthy European hunters owned an extensive collection of dogs that included pointers to locate game, setters to retrieve, and hounds to trail quarry over long distances. These wealthy landowners would hunt on their property, and bring these dogs with them. The Vizsla became even more essential when firearms proliferated in the 18th century.

The Vizsla survived the Hungarian Revolution of 1848, and World War I. However, perhaps the biggest threat to the existence of the Vizsla was the onslaught of World War II. When Russian forces invaded Hungary, it caused many of the wealthy aristocrats to escape their land. They fled to other parts of Europe and North America, smuggling their Vizslas and pedigree records out of the country. The present-day Vizslas descended from this small stock of dogs that survived World War II.

As World War II ended, the Vizsla started to arrive in the United States. The breed saw an increase in interest and devotion by dog owners, and soon the Vizsla Club of America was formed, to gain the recognition of the American Kennel Club. Vizsla owners were officially recognized in 1960 as a result of registering foundation stock with the AKC. The Vizsla became the 115th breed to be recognized by the AKC.

Vizslas, The Hungarian Hunting Dogs

'Vizsla' means pointer in Hungarian, which aptly describes the dog's remarkable skill in pointing fowls and game during hunts. The Magyar tribe worked closely with them for trailing and retrieving their hunt target.

The Vizsla is one of the best close-working gun dogs. It can run all day and has an exceptional nose that is capable of tracking fowl and game. It can perform outstandingly, in a range of terrain. It is also an excellent swimmer and can retrieve game, even on water. It can also quickly adapt to different hunting strategies, such as pheasant or quail hunting. It can hunt sharp-tails on open prairies, as well as grouse in thick woods.

Indeed, this dog breed is a certified hunter and a talented pointer. There is no doubt why hunters choose the Vizsla to be their companions.

How Can A Vizsla Fit Into Your Life and Family?

The Vizsla's size is one of its most attractive characteristics, as it is one of the smaller-sized hunting dogs. For many centuries, this breed has been a highly favored sporting dog, and now, has become a beloved household companion and family dog. The Vizsla desires to be a close member of the family that owns him.

This dog breed was nurtured for many centuries to become close companions to their owners. Hence, they do not like to be "put in the kennel" with the other dogs. They will most likely prefer to share a bed with you, and behave as though they have equal rights with other members of your family, if you let them. They have the reputation of being "Velcro" dogs, which means they will always be by your side, and will never leave you when you are around.

If you start off on the right foot in socializing your Vizsla, you can assure good behavior around children and visitors. They love to play and show their affection and energy. You still need to monitor your Vizsla around toddlers, as too much excitement will cause your dog to knock over little kids by accident. Teach younger kids first how to approach the Vizsla so they can safely pet them without hurting or startling the dog.

If you are considering getting a Vizsla, you must keep in mind that this dog needs plenty of exercise and proper training. You need to be committed to providing this for your Vizsla.

With their royal bloodline and pedigree, Vizslas are well-mannered dogs that definitely love to be in the presence of their family, and are a delight to own.

Vizsla Competitions

One of the competitions you can enter your Vizsla into is the AKC Field Trials. These are hunting matches where the handler can actively participate with the dog. The dogs run in braces (pairs) for 20-30 minutes over a course where birds have been set loose. They must meet minimum performance requirements and outdo other dogs that are entered in the same stake (class) for it to be considered awarded a placement.

The Field Trials are one of the most esteemed competitions for hunting dogs. It is usually organized by kennel clubs or other gun dog organizations. The dogs may compete with other breeds, or the host club may only allow Vizslas to participate. There are different levels of competition – juvenile and adult, and various categories (Puppy, Derby, Gun Dog, Limited Gun Dog, and All-Age). The Field Trials have evolved to test the working ability of Gundogs. They simulate actual competitive conditions and closely emulate a day's hunting in the field. There are different kinds of game that the dogs in the competition are expected to handle: from rabbits, hares, partridges, and pheasants.

Other competitions that test the Vizsla's agility, athletic build, and hunting ability are Point Score Competitions. Both the owner and the dog can participate in this sport. It is widely organized in Australia and the United States. In this competition, Vizslas compete with each other within age categories. The dogs are judged on different criteria. A dog is awarded the championship when it has gained the highest total number of points.

The Tracking Test has the Vizsla take charge, as opposed to the owner ordering a dog to perform a task. This sport allows the dog to perform its natural instinct of following a person or animal by using its nose to identify the scent. Dog and owner teams are recognized in four titles: Tracking Dog (TD), Tracking Dog Excellent, Variable Surface Tracking (VST), and Champion Tracker (CT).

Obedience Tests are also a great way to evaluate how the owner has trained his dog. Owners must train their dogs in heelwork, recall, retrieve, send-aways, stays, scent discrimination, and distance control. Another obedience competition is the Rally. Any dog breed can enter this contest, but this is one the Vizsla can really excel in. This involves the owner and the dog working as a team to go through an obstacle course. At each stop, there is a designated task to be performed.

Vizsla Dog Breed Standards and How to Identify a Purebred Vizsla

The Vizsla is a medium-sized dog with a robust but light build.

The Official Standard is a document that serves as the basis for the standard of the characteristics and appearance by which an ideal Vizsla is measured. The official breed standards by the American Kennel Club are drafted from the parent breed clubs. This is also used by AKC judges in identifying dogs that closely conform to the breed standard. The standard serves as a guideline for breeders to select the best dog of their particular breed. This is to improve the breeding stock and performance. The information that the breed standard presents will also help new owners assess dogs when selecting one.

The following breed standards are the ideal characteristics of a Vizsla. Any difference or deviation from the specified qualities is often disqualified or penalized. Other extreme deviations that affect the Vizsla's performance and function, are considered as severe penalties. Those that only affect the appearance, cause less of a penalty.

General Appearance

The Vizsla is a medium-sized dog with a robust, but light build. It appears brawny and sinewy and in muscular condition. Its coat is short, and the color is usually an attractive shade of golden rust.

Size and Weight

The ideal size for male Vizslas is 22 to 24 inches (56 to 61 centimeters) measured from the highest point over the shoulder blades. For females, the size is 21 to 23 inches (53 to 58 centimeters). Vizslas are recognized as medium-sized hunting breeds. Dogs entered into show competitions that are more than 1 ½ inches (3.8 centimeters) over or under these dimensions, are disqualified.

The ideal weight for male Vizslas ranges between 46 to 65 pounds (21 to 29 kilograms). The females' weight can be lesser, between 40 to 55 pounds (18 to 25 kilograms).

Coat

The Vizsla's coat is short, smooth, dense, and close-lying. It does not have any wooly undercoat. Vizslas with a distinctly long coat are considered not a purebred one.

Color

The Vizsla's coat color is golden rust, in varying shades. There are lighter shadings over the sides of the neck and shoulders. This somehow gives an appearance that there is a "saddle" placed on the dog. If there is a white coloration that can be seen, it must appear as small as possible. Visible white markings should only be confined to an area on top of the sternum to a point between the elbows. White markings that can be seen on the shoulders or neck, disqualify the dog. The Vizsla's coat is self-colored, with the color of the eyes, eye-rims, lips, nose, toenails, and pads of the feet matching the color of the coat. The dog is disqualified from meeting the breed standard if it shows different colors and markings on its coat.

Head

The Vizsla's head is lean and muscular. The skull is moderately broad between the ears, and a median line can be seen down the forehead. When viewed in profile, the muzzle or foreface is equal in length or slightly shorter than the skull. Its thickness should also gradually reduce from the top to the tip of the nose. The muzzle is also square, deep, and should not turn up like a "dish", nor should it turn down.

The whiskers (vibrissae is the more accurate term) have many functions that help the dog in hunting. Their removal or trimming is permitted, but not preferred. However, for some dog shows, this may be a cause for disqualification.

In the nose area, the nostrils are slightly open. The color is reddish, a similar shade to the coat. If you see a Vizsla with its nose having a different color (like black, brown, or light pink), it is indicative that it is not a purebred dog and has been mixed with another breed. This differing color in the nose can result in disqualification in dog shows.

The ears are thin, silky, and proportionately long. They have rounded-leather ends, and is set relatively low and hanging close to the cheeks.

The eyes are medium in size and are set deep in the skull. The color of the iris is similar and should blend with the coat. Any other color of the eyes, such as yellow, indicates that it is not a purebred Vizsla. The surrounding tissues of the eyes cover the white areas. The lower eyelids should not turn in or out. If you see your dog having this eye condition, this may increase the likelihood of irritation from seeds and dust.

The Vizsla should have strong and well-developed jaws. Its teeth are white and should come in contact with a scissors bite. The lips fully and snugly cover the jaws, not too loose or floppy.

Neck and Body

The Vizsla's neck is strong, smooth, and sinewy. It is moderately long and arched. It also does not have any dewlap and broadens nicely to the shoulders, which are also somewhat laid back. These characteristics are important to keep the Vizsla's balance, and to complement its angulated hindquarters.

The Vizsla's body is well-proportioned and sturdy. The dog may appear square in shape, but it is slightly longer than tall when measured from the breastbone to the buttocks, and from the highest point of the shoulder blades to the ground. Proportion is the keyword when evaluating a Vizsla. If it has met the ideal standard, it must not appear long and low, or tall and leggy.

The Vizsla's backline is firm, with a slight rise over a short and brawny loin. The dog's croup (the top line of the hindquarters) is gently rounded to the base of the tail. It is also not steep, sunken, or flat. A proportionately-built Vizsla maintains a steady and level backline when moving at a trot.

The chest is moderately broad and deep, reaching down to the elbows. Its ribs are well-sprung. The tail is located just below the croup, thicker at the base, and docked one-third off. The tail should ideally reach the stifle joint, and when it is moving, it should move horizontally. It must not stay in a vertical position, curled over the back, or hang between the legs. A docked tail is preferred.

Forequarters

The Vizsla's shoulder blades are proportionately long and wide. You can also see a moderate slope at the back. Its upper arm is almost equal in length to the shoulder blade. This allows for good extension. Its forelegs are straight and muscular, with the elbows close.

Its feet are cat-like, round and compact with the toes close. The pads are thick and tough. If it were not for its nails hitting the floor, you would not hear a Vizsla walking at all. The nails are brown and short. To prevent your Vizsla from getting injuries when running in the field, it is recommended that you remove its dewclaws on the front and rear of the feet.

Hindquarters

The dog's hind legs are well-developed. The thighs and stifles are moderately angulated. These parts are well-balanced with the shoulders, which are moderately laid back. They must appear straight when you look at it from behind. The hocks are set down and must be parallel to each other. The Vizsla will not adhere to the standard quality if there is too much difference in the angle at the hocks.

Gait

The Vizsla's stride is far-reaching, graceful, and smooth. It is also light-footed and creates minimal noise- if it were not for its nails. An ideally-built Vizsla moves in a single track when it is trotting at a fast pace.

Temperament

This breed is lively, gentle-mannered, and demonstrates affectionate and sensitive behavior. It is a courageous dog that exhibits fearlessness while showing a well-developed protective instinct. It is considered a penalty, and a cause for disqualification when a Vizsla shows signs of shyness, timidity or nervousness.

CHAPTER 2
Knowing Your Vizsla

Vizslas are known as "Velcro dogs," which means they need to be together with their owners, the majority of the time. It is recommended that a Vizsla is owned by a family or a person who can be present most of the time. Vizslas may exhibit signs of stress or separation anxiety when they do not spend enough time with you, or when you are away for a long period of time. They express this through destructive chewing and excessive howling or barking.

Vizsla Behavior

Vizslas are very vocal and verbal dogs who like to be heard. You may think your Vizsla is trying to communicate with you by barking, howling, grunting, whining, moaning, and making "talking" noises the entire day. They also are very prone to excessive barking, and it is imperative to train your Vizsla to obey commands that tone down their volume. A Vizsla may not be the dog for you if you are looking for one that can stay silent, or be left alone for an extended period.

The Vizsla is a highly energetic breed that needs an owner that can match its stamina!

Vizsla Temperament

The Vizsla is a highly energetic breed that needs an owner that can match its stamina. It displays overprotective behavior and an endearing streak. The Vizsla is also a versatile dog that you can train as a watch or guard dog. It is quick to bark but is friendly to visitors. If you are an outgoing person who usually has guests at home, this dog won't give you too many problems- as they love the company of people.

The Vizsla is also known for its loyal affection and mild demeanor. It is very personable and loving towards its owners. It is easy to socialize a Vizsla as it too loves to make new friends, but they will always remain loyal to their families. This remarkable loyalty proves that Vizslas can become your perfect companion.

Vizsla Personality

For many years, the Vizsla has been trained to remain by its owner's side during hunts. This proximity and activities have created a strong bond with humans and has been carried on by generations of Vizslas.

This breed is a fit, active, and lively one, who loves to explore and exercise. Expect the Vizsla to enthusiastically participate in activities such as running, playing games, and swimming. It is the top dog when it comes to canine sports such as agility, obedience, and heelwork. The Vizsla is a happy and outgoing dog with lots of energy to expend. Perhaps the only time a Vizsla keeps still is when it is lounging with its owner!

The Versatile Vizsla

The Vizsla is an excellent active and outdoor companion, but will also love to snuggle with you on a lazy day. It can also provide you with practical service if trained well. It can work as a therapy, guide, search, and rescue, and drug detection dog. Its exceptional skill in scent tracking makes it the ideal dog to perform these tasks.

Vizsla Breed – Is This the Right One for You and Your Family?

The Vizsla is suited to belong to a family with an active lifestyle. They are excellent dogs to accompany you in hiking, biking, and jogging trips. The hunting field is where they truly shine and where you can see the Vizsla perform extraordinary skills in pointing and retrieving.

If you are considering owning a Vizsla, you must be prepared to spend at least an hour per day exercising and running it. You will also need a vast space to let your Vizsla run and stretch its muscular legs, so you may want to think carefully if you live in a city with few parks or green spaces.

They are also one of the best breeds to introduce to children, especially if you're teaching your kids responsible pet ownership. They love to play with children of all ages and always look forward to being included in every aspect of family life. The Vizsla's gentle personality will make it easy for children to socialize, without worrying about the dog harming them.
The Vizsla is eager to please people, unlike other breeds that attempt to dominate children, as they do in a pack. They are not aggressive, snappy, or rough with children and can play with them without inflicting any harm.

Vizslas are friendly and can easily socialize with other dogs. It is best, however, to start socializing them when they are still puppies. They rarely become aggressive or show dominance. They can also comfortably fit in, if you have other breeds of dogs living in your home, and would even treat them as their family or pack.

Is the Vizsla Hypoallergenic? – Good News for Your Family

Families who have members that are prone to allergic reactions are drawn to owning a dog that is hypoallergenic. But what exactly triggers an allergic reaction from dogs?

Allergy Triggers

Often, an allergic reaction is caused by a protein found in the dog's saliva and skin cells. These are also abundantly supplied in the dog's dander, the loose scales that can form on the skin and is shed from the coat. These skin flakes may sometimes be trapped in the dog's fur, and when it shakes, it scatters them in the air along with some loose fur. This floating allergen can cause you to start sneezing, itching, and making your eyes water.

Hypoallergenic Dogs

No dog is completely hypoallergenic, but dogs with short coats are more so. These qualities lessen the amount of fur expelled into the air and helps prevent allergic reactions. These types of dogs also produce less dander, which means lesser skin flakes and reaction-causing proteins that you may inhale from these dogs.

Vizslas As Hypoallergenic Dogs

With its short fur and lack of undercoat, Vizslas are an excellent choice, if you are looking for a dog that is somewhat hypoallergenic. Undercoats are fine; they are fluffy hairs that grow closest to the dog's skin and usually provide the best defense against chilly temperatures. This may be good news for families who don't want to worry about allergic reactions, but you also need to consider the Vizsla's needs and protect it from extreme temperatures. The lack of undercoat means the Vizsla is more susceptible to the effects of cold temperatures, which could result in hypothermia. It is highly advised that you do not leave a Vizsla outside at night. You also need to consider keeping your Vizsla warm during winter, or any other icy weather conditions. Allow your Vizsla to come inside your house, to keep it warm.

Vizsla Life Expectancy and Stages

The Vizsla's average lifespan is 11 to 15 years.

Its life stage starts at birth up to the first three weeks. The Vizsla is still a puppy that is born blind, deaf, and with only soft gums. A newborn puppy's weight will typically range from 0.5-0.85 pounds (0.23-0.4 kilograms). It will depend much on its mom for nutrition and warmth. By the second week, the Vizsla puppy starts to become more mobile. Movements will involve crawling and pushing itself around. Nearing the third week, the Vizsla puppy will begin to open its eyes, and its ears will also start to open. Little teeth will also emerge. The Vizsla puppy will become more active and aware of the world around it and will begin walking, barking, and playing with its littermates.

The second stage starts at three to seven weeks. The puppy will grow more in size and weight, where it can gain about a pound per week. Its milk teeth will start coming out, and it will begin weaning. At this stage, the pup will also learn about bite inhibition (controlling the force of the bite), and 'pecking order' (order of dominance in the litter) is established. Slowly, the pup can be left alone to eat dry puppy food. By week six or seven, the Vizsla puppy's brain has grown to 70% of adult brain size. This is also an excellent time to have its first set of vaccinations and deworming.

The third stage is marked by the 7th to the 12th week of the Vizsla's life. The puppy can now be separated from its mom and littermates and can be introduced to its new human family. Bonds can usually be formed at around the 8th to the 9th week. You need to note, however, that your puppy may experience the "fear period" where it will feel apprehensive and anxious towards its new surroundings. Slowly socialize it with the members of your family, and allow it to feel welcome and safe. This is also the perfect time to start training your Vizsla.

The fourth stage is marked by the 12th to the 16th week, and this will be a more chaotic period in the Vizsla puppy's life, if you aren't able to get it under control. The pup will start teething and will feel soreness in its gums. In an attempt to alleviate the pain, the puppy will chew on anything that it comes across. Provide the dog with toys that are safe to chew on.

Your Vizsla puppy will continue to grow at a rapid rate when it enters the fifth stage of its life (17 to 40 weeks). Permanent teeth are setting in, which you need now to help maintain, by brushing its teeth. By eight months the dog should be capable of holding its bladder and bowel, so make efficient use of this time to potty train your dog. By the 9th month, your Vizsla will become sexually mature and will continue to reach its optimal size until the 18th month.

The sixth stage is marked when your Vizsla pup has lived for a year. It may show signs of stubbornness, and the best way to counter this is to continue obedience training. You need to assert your dominance as the leader of the pack, and use a firm voice when commanding your dog.

The Vizsla has reached full maturity when it is more than a year old. This is the time when your Vizsla will demand more time to engage in vigorous exercise. You will need to channel this energy outdoors, or else you will end up with a house that has been damaged by a bored Vizsla! This is also the stage when you should consider having your Vizsla spayed or neutered.

CHAPTER 3

Vizsla Dog Training for Beginners

The Vizsla is a highly intelligent dog with an excellent memory. Because it is eager to please its owners, the dog is very responsive to handling and training. They are also very sensitive, and must be trained with patience and positive reinforcement.

The Vizsla is a highly intelligent dog with an excellent memory.

It is ideal to start training your Vizsla when it is still a puppy. This is the prime season for your dog to absorb what you teach it and establish good habits and behavior.

How to Train a Vizsla

Respect is the most critical attitude you must build in your Vizsla, during its puppyhood. It must be able to recognize your authority and dominance, or else it will become unruly and ignore the things you want it to do. You might also fail to bring out the Vizsla's full potential of being an excellent partner if you won't deal with its behavior when it is still young.

The best way to train your Vizsla puppy is to start with word commands. This is the foundational component of training before you can move on to other tasks that you want your Vizsla to perform. The key is to be consistent with your instructions.

What and How to Prepare When Training a Vizsla

You need ample space when training your Vizsla. These dogs are excellent runners, and they need enough room to sprint at full speed. A house with a big yard can also be an ideal place for your Vizsla to start. If you are living in the city, however, it might be best if you can find a way to take it out to the park.

Some items that you can get before training your Vizsla are:

- **Chain slide collar.** When choosing a chain, a medium link works best. You must be able to put the collar over the dog's head, and it must fit snugly under the dog's chin. It must not be looser than 4 inches (10 centimeters). This will enable you to make quick corrections without inflicting injuries to your dog. You can, however, leave this when you're out in the field training your Vizsla.

- **Lead (or leash).** The ideal length is 6 feet (183 centimeters), and the width is 3/8 inches (9 centimeters). The leather is a more flexible material than nylon.
- **Treats.** This is part of positive reinforcement. Reward your dog with treats when it has successfully performed a task. Small soft treats work best when training your dog.
- **Pen/Kennel/Crate.** You may need this if you need to travel with your dog for long distances, and also this is pivotal to crate training of course.
- **Water.** Always have a supply of water ready for your Vizsla. You may consider bringing a portable dog bowl and water container.

Dominance and Obedience Training – How to Do This With Your Vizsla?

Vizslas respond well to obedience training. One thing you'll need to deal with, however, is how to prevent the Vizsla from getting distracted. Remember not to be harsh with your Vizsla, and punishing it when the dog fails to obey your commands. They quickly learn more through positive reinforcement by rewarding it with treats when it has correctly performed the task you want it to learn at a particular training session.

You can start obedience training with your Vizsla with the following commands:

Sit

You can start by holding a treat close to your dog's nose and letting it be acquainted with the scent. Next, while still grasping the treat, slowly raise your hand, making sure that its head is following your motion. If correctly done, the dog will lower its bottom half. Once it is in a sitting position, say "Sit." If your Vizsla has successfully demonstrated this, give the treat and show it praise and affection. This command is important if you need your dog to be calm and seated.

Down

This is also helpful when you need your Vizsla to stay for a period of time. Use a tasty and enjoyable smelling treat, and grasp it with a closed fist. Move your hand close to your dog's nose, and allow it to smell the treat inside your hand. Slowly move your hand to the floor and let your dog follow your movement. Slide your hand along the ground in front of the dog; this will encourage it to lower its body. Once it is in the position, say "Down," and reward it with the treat and show praise. Do this daily until your Vizsla understands the command. Don't force it to lower its body by pushing it down. When your Vizsla lunges at your hand to take the treat, immediately move your hand away and say "no."

Stay

Make sure your Vizsla has mastered the command "sit" before moving on to "stay." This is helpful in keeping your Vizsla still and preventing it from sprinting away even before you get ready.

Make your Vizsla "sit," then open the palm of your hand in front of you, and say "Stay." Slowly distance yourself by taking a few steps back. When the dog stays, give him a treat as a reward, and show praise. Once your Vizsla is starting to understand this command, increase the number of steps you take.

You will need to repeat this for a few times daily until your dog has mastered it. The next part of this training is teaching the dog to sit during particular times of the day. An example of this is at mealtimes, and before going out for walks.

Come

There will be times you need your Vizsla to come to you to prevent it from getting lost and in danger. This is where this command is useful.

To start, fit a collar and leash on your dog. Distance yourself from the dog a few paces away. Lower yourself to its level and say, "Come," while gently pulling on the leash. When it goes near you, give the treat as a reward and praise your dog.

Once your Vizsla has mastered this command with the leash, you may move on to removing it and practicing the command in a safe, enclosed area.

Vizsla Training in the Field – How Can You Start?

Before going out with your Vizsla for field training, there are some items that you need to have to make training easier:

For Your Vizsla

- **Buckle collar.** A strap buckle collar works best. Make sure it fits comfortably on your Vizsla, and allows for some room to "breathe" when it is out running on the field. Never use a chain choker collar during field training.

- **Orange and yellow reversible field collar.** This will enable you to spot your Vizsla in tall grasses. It is also used to identify dogs during field events.
- **Leash.** This is to keep your dog in place before starting your training
- **Long line or check cord.** The ideal cord length is 8 to 10 feet (244 to 305 centimeters). This allows your dog to move within a further range, while maintaining control. This will also make you ready to give corrections.

For Owners

- **Orange vest or shirt.** This is for your Vizsla to be able to see you when out in the field. The AKC also requires owners to wear this garment, especially when live ammunition is being used.
- **Whistle.** A standard referee's whistle will suffice. You will need this when calling your dog's attention, especially when it has moved far away from you.
- **Durable shoes.** You need a pair that can withstand different types and levels of terrain.
- **Sun protection.** Put on a hat, sunscreen, or a pair of sunglasses. The sun's rays and heat may affect you during training.
- **Leather gloves.** In case your Vizsla needs rescuing when it gets trapped in tall grasses and thorns, you need to protect your hands from getting injured. A pair will also prevent rope burn when you're grasping a long line or cord.

- **Starter Pistol 22 caliber.** Since the Vizsla is a gun dog and is instinctively a hunter, it needs to be introduced and be accustomed to working with a gun. Never fire a shot close to your dog or a brace mate. This is for more experienced handlers and Vizsla trainers. The utmost care and precaution are expected when handling this tool. Ensure that you carry it in a holster around your waist for safety.

Essential Items

- **First aid kit.** Remember that you will be out on the field and anything can happen that may cause injury to you or your Vizsla. Immediate medical attention may be far away from you. Some items you need to include are bandages, gauze, medical tape, scissors, hydrogen peroxide, antibiotic ointment, towel, and antiseptic wipes.
- **Tweezers.** A thorn may get lodged in your skin or your Vizsla's pads and may be buried deeper and cause infections. Use tweezers to pull any thorns out immediately.
- **Water supply.** You need to prevent dehydration and overheating at all costs. This can be fatal for you and your Vizsla. A big bottle is ideal, and remember to keep it filled before going to the field for training.
- **Food.** Make sure you have enough supply to sustain you, and your Vizsla's energy, during training. Consider bringing a collapsible dog bowl for your Vizsla to use during meal time.
- **AKC Pointing Breed Hunting Test Rule Book.** This book will educate you about the standards of field training. This will help you to learn about best practices that are observed at a competition level.

Vizsla Hunt Field Commands

- **"Whoa" (Stop).** A good place to train your Vizsla to obey this command is in your backyard. Put the leash on your dog first before starting. Move around the area a few times. Make a sudden stop while firmly saying "Woah" and jerking on the leash. Make sure your dog halts and stays in a standing position. When your Vizsla has successfully done this, stroke its back and praise it for a job well done. Continue to do this daily until your Vizsla has mastered this command and work on this to the point where you can remove the leash.
- **"Fetch" and Retrieve.** Mastery of this command will enable your Vizsla to retrieve game and fowl you have hunted out in the field. Attach the leash on your Vizsla and let it stay by your side. Start by throwing a ball out a few feet away from you and the dog. Don't let it run after the ball until you have said: "fetch." Allow your Vizsla to retrieve the ball while you grasp the leash, so you can gently pull it back to your position once it has caught the ball. If your Vizsla successfully brings the ball back to you, give a reward, and show praise. Practice this 5 to 10 times daily with your dog and work on it until you can remove the leash from your Vizsla.
- **"Up."** This position allows your Vizsla to stay alert and ready for your next command. To do this, let your Vizsla run on a long leash. Move ahead of your dog and say "up" while reeling it towards you. Keep moving forward, but adjust your pace accordingly so your Vizsla can keep up with you.
- Other commands from the obedience training will also work well in the field, such as "sit," "stay," and "come."

Vizsla Hunting Training – What Do You and Your Dog Need to Achieve?

Your goal when starting your Vizsla hunting training is for the dog to show a keen interest to hunt. It must be able to display boldness, independence, speed, and an efficient running pattern.

Back Course

Keep a reasonable distance between you and your Vizsla when you start.

Allow your Vizsla to start looking for the game by letting it approach bushes, grass clumps, and other spots where birds gather. Give the dog time to sniff these areas. When it has successfully found a target, give rewards and positive reinforcement.

Be assertive with your dog if it is trailing, bumping, or getting distracted. Command its attention if needed.

Bird Finding Ability

You need to identify the behaviors a Vizsla will exhibit when it has found a scent. It will come at a slower pace and may approach the same area several times. Its body will tense up, and it will creep along into the scent cone, as it comes closer to the game. Use a check cord to keep your Vizsla steady and prevent it from lunging at the target.

Gun Response

To train your Vizsla to get accustomed to you using a gun during hunting training, start by letting it run at a distance. Once there is a considerable range between you and the dog, fire the pistol aimed at the horizon. Assess your Vizsla's reaction and make sure it does not display signs of anxiety as you get closer working with the gun. Your goal is to be able to fire the pistol with the Vizsla near you.

Other Good Behaviors That You Can Train Your Vizsla To Perform

Crate Training

When your Vizsla is properly house trained, this will save you a lot of time and energy in the long run.

This skill is important for your Vizsla to master to make transportation easier and safer. It is ideal to start your Vizsla with this training while it is still a puppy. The goal is to make your dog comfortable going into and staying in a crate. When your dog is properly crate trained, it can bring other benefits such as keeping it out of mischief, and reduce excessive barking and digging. It can also be a method to potty-train your Vizsla, as it will consider the crate to be its bed. Dogs usually won't soil the places where they sleep.

You will need to get a wire cage or an airline crate to do this training. Never force and push your dog inside the crate. You must create a fun experience for your dog as it enters the crate. You may do this by throwing treats and toys inside, and allow the dog to enter on its own. While your dog is entering the crate, accompany a command to give it the signal such as "go inside" or "in." Remember to be consistent with your command.

Your dog must see the crate as a haven where it can feel a sense of security, and have some quiet time. Never use it as a form of punishment, or create an association that a crate is a place of negativity and anger.

Never place the crate inside the shed or garage, as this will make your Vizsla feel isolated. You can position it somewhere inside your home, where it can still approach you and the family if it wants to.

Housebreaking Training

Properly house training your Vizsla will save you a lot of time and energy in the long run. Instilling some essential housebreaking habits can help you train your Vizsla in going outside to potty. One routine you can establish is letting your dog go out through the door after its meal. It will also be ideal if you can designate a specific spot where your dog can come back to when doing its business. Remember to use positive reinforcement such as rewarding it with treats, and giving praises when it has successfully relieved itself on the location you have specified.

Bladder and bowel control

There will be times your dog needs to relieve itself, and your current location is not the ideal place for it to do its business. That is why you need to teach your Vizsla how to control its bladder and bowel. This will go well with crate training, as dogs instinctively avoid leaving their waste in areas where they sleep. However, don't leave your dog inside for too long where it cannot hold its bladder or bowel anymore.

How to Become a Vizsla Savvy Owner

Be Consistent

You need to establish a training routine for your Vizsla and commit to it. Only give treats as rewards when it has obeyed your commands and has performed well. You also need to be consistent with your verbal and non-verbal language. Don't change the terms you say as you command your dog. Your body language should also reflect how you feel towards your Vizsla at any given moment, so the dog will show its respect and obedience to you.

Look Out for Training Opportunities

When you live with your Vizsla in an area that does not afford you to go out to the field, and your next best pick is the park, look out for opportunities where your Vizsla can practice its hunting skills. During walks, you may notice your Vizsla circling a spot in the park or at other public places numerous times. Try to be patient and see what your Vizsla is tracking. Remember that it is important to allow it to naturally track a smell, and not to pull a hunting dog off-scent.

Use Visual Commands

You may also consider using visual commands, such as pointing to a direction where a game or fowl can potentially be found. Remember that this will only serve as a guide for your Vizsla to track a scent. Ideally, it will move in a zig-zag motion towards the source of the scent.

Get the Right Tools

Vizsla training will be a lot easier and efficient if you already have all the tools you need before you even start. You can maintain the training momentum, and you and your dog will be able to adjust to the tools as the training progresses.

Grow with Your Vizsla

Remember that as you go on through the process of training, you and your Vizsla will improve and learn to handle specific tasks together. Each of you will develop through constant practice and learning from your experiences.

Whether you are keen on training your Vizsla to be a good house companion, or to become the great hunter that it is, it takes commitment. You would not want to waste its high intelligence and excellent potential!

CHAPTER 4

Vizsla Puppy or Adult; Male or Female: What and How to Choose for Your Family

You need to understand that a puppy and an adult dog have different needs and the way you take care of them. Their temperament and behavior will also be different.

Vizsla Puppy or Adult – Which Should You Choose?

Puppies

If you choose to go with a Vizsla puppy, you'll be starting with a clean slate. You will have the responsibility of training and teaching it all the skills it needs to learn to be able to live with you. You will also create a stronger bond with your Vizsla puppy, compared to getting an adult one. At an early age, you can train the puppy to see you as the leader, as well as cultivating respect that the dog needs to show you. This is a necessary foundation when you start training your puppy.

Vizslas are inherently affectionate dogs, so it won't be a problem forming a strong bond for life.

On the other hand, puppies can be unruly and are prone to misbehaving, such as chewing your furniture and urinating all over the place. They have little control over their bowel and bladder at first, so expect to see them take potty breaks every few hours. If you fail to train them early on, they will carry bad habits into adulthood, and it may be difficult to correct them when they become older. Puppies have a shorter attention span, so you will need to have lots of patience when dealing with them.

When you do choose to get a Vizsla puppy, never get one that is under seven weeks old. The pup is still very much dependent on its mother and needs all the nutrients that it can get from her. It is also during this time that it gets to learn fundamental disciplines such as bite inhibition, where the mother will shake or nip the puppy once it starts to bite too hard. It has been seen that puppies separated from their mothers before seven weeks exhibit problematic behaviors when they are with other dogs.

You need to make sure that a Vizsla puppy is eight to twelve weeks old, before bringing it home. Age 8-12 weeks old, is also the time you will be able to begin house training your Vizsla puppy.

Adults

Vizslas are in the adult stage when they reach one year. Getting an adult Vizsla dog means that you are accepting it as it is. You may not entirely know what the dog has been through, and its background may have positive and negative experiences. This may pose a problem when it is socializing with other people. You need to be observant of how your dog would react in the presence of men, women, children, and other animals, and form a baseline of its behavior.

Contrary to popular belief, you can teach dogs new tricks! Vizslas are highly intelligent dogs that are eager to learn new things and please their owners. Adult dogs can keep their attention longer compared to puppies, which will be easier when teaching it commands. It may be hard, however, to change the Vizsla's established habits. It can become resistant to change, so you would need to get your Vizsla from an owner whom you know, or a rescue group that has been able to observe the dog's habits for a substantial amount of time.

Vizslas are inherently affectionate dogs, so it won't be a problem to form a bond with your adult Vizsla.

You must be prepared to take care of any health issues that come as your dog ages. If you have a purebred Vizsla, you should always assume that it is inbred, to a certain extent. This means that the dog's parents are closely related to each other genetically. The recessive mutations caused by inbreeding can pose a lot of health threats for your Vizsla.

Vizsla Male or Female – What's the Best One for You?

The Vizsla's gender will also be a factor that you need to consider.

Males

Males can be more aggressive and bolder. A study conducted by the University of Minnesota, about dog bite injuries and fatalities in the United States, shows that males are six times more likely to bite than female dogs.

He will also have a larger build and appear more muscular. This is something you may want to consider if you're looking for a Vizsla that will work and provide service for you.

Females

Female dogs are seen as more affectionate. They are less aggressive, but they can be moody. It also costs more to spay a female dog than to neuter a male dog. When your bitch reaches sexual maturity, it will excrete menstrual blood. This may occur every six months and starts when your bitch is between 12 to 18 months. You may be alarmed to see blood droplets on the floor; the color can be deep red, pink, or clear. If your bitch conceives and gets pregnant, you will need to take care of her and assist her during delivery day. Since you will be owning a female Vizsla, you will also be responsible for taking care of her puppies in their early stages, if you allow her to get pregnant.

If you enter your female Vizsla in competitions, her performance may be affected (or not be able to participate at all) when she gets pregnant, and after she has given birth to the puppies.

Vizsla Purebred or Mixed Breed – Which Should You Choose?

Purebred Vizslas

If you choose to get a purebred Vizsla, you must be prepared for the possible health threats that it may experience. First, you need to understand how a purebred dog comes to exist. The parents or grandparents of purebred dogs are most often closely related to each other genetically. This is done with the goal of producing puppies that are consistent in appearance, temperament, and ability.

This closed-breeding with its fellow genetic relative, however, means that there is no new genetic material introduced to the dog's family. As some dogs do not reproduce, the gene pool decreases. The next generation of puppies is also prone to exhibit detrimental recessive genes that can potentially cause severe abnormalities and diseases. There is a risk of two disease-causing genes to pair and proliferate. If mated with other dogs of the same species, this condition may be inherited by the puppies.

If you aim to acquire a Vizsla that meets dog-show standards, be sure to get one that is registered in a Kennel Club.

Mixed Breed Vizslas

A mixed breed Vizsla is produced when you take one purebred Vizsla and mate it with another different purebred dog of a different breed.

A mixed-breed Vizsla is produced when you take one purebred Vizsla and mate it with another different purebred dog of a different breed. Some Vizsla mixed breeds that have emerged are the Labrador Retriever mix, Weimaraner mix, German Shepherd mix, and the Pitbull mix.

Mixed-breed Vizslas will have an increased chance of carrying healthier genes. This potentially contributes to a more robust immune system and can contribute to better physical and mental health.

It will, however, possess a moderate temperament – a result of the parents of different breeds endowing their traits onto their puppies. You may not expect a mixed breed Vizsla to perform and behave the same way as a purebred dog.

CHAPTER 5

Buying vs. Adopting a Vizsla- Which is Right For You?

There are two main options for how you can get your Vizsla: by purchase or adoption. If you're planning to buy a Vizsla, responsible dog breeders or Kennel Clubs are the best choices to get one. If you are planning to adopt, you need to search for rescue groups in your area. But, what are the pros and cons of each option, and what should you keep in mind?

Buying a Vizsla vs. Adopting– Which Should You Choose?

Buying

The real definition of a "dog breeder" is a person who owns a female dog who has a litter. A responsible dog breeder should have the following documents:

- A certificate from the Canine Eye Registry Foundation (CERF) – dated within the past year – certifying the dog to be free of eye diseases.

- A certificate from the Orthopedic Foundation of America (OFA) or PennHip, certifying the dog has no abnormalities with its hips.
- A certificate from the Orthopedic Foundation of America (OFA), certifying the dog to have a normal thyroid.

The seller should be able to show you the abovementioned certificates. Otherwise, your Vizsla might be at high risk of health problems. If you decide to go ahead and purchase a Vizsla without seeing these certificates, you need to be prepared to respond to any health complications. Some of these health issues include cataracts, thyroid disease, and bad hip joints.

Responsible breeders would also want their pup to go to a responsible owner. Expect a breeder to ask you the questions below:

- Where did you hear about Vizslas?
- What are your expectations for the dog?
- What particular characteristics are you looking for?
- Why do you want a Vizsla, and not another breed or a mixed breed?
- What are your prior experiences with dogs/Vizslas, especially training them?
- Have you ever raised a puppy before?
- How many people are living in your home, (adults and children), and what are their ages?
- What is your lifestyle like, and how will the dog fit into it? Is someone at home during the day?

- Are there other pets in the house?
- Do you intend to spay/neuter or breed your dog?
- What kind of dwelling do you live in? Do you have a fenced yard, and if not, where do you plan to have the dog get its daily exercise?
- Are you interested in showing your dog, or co-owning with the breeder until show qualities are or are not obvious?
- What is your current veterinarian's name and phone number?

Never buy from sellers who post on advertisements, or pet stores–good breeders have a waiting list for their puppies.

Adopting

Rescued Vizslas are turned over to shelters or rescue groups where they can receive care and attention.

Unfortunately, there are Vizslas that have been neglected by their owners. Some dogs are given up by families because of circumstances, or they see that they cannot anymore provide for the Vizsla's needs. In such cases, these dogs are turned over to shelters or rescue groups, where they can receive care and attention. Adopting a dog is the more ethical choice because you get to save the dog's life and provide it with a home, and another chance for it to become a part of a family.

Vizsla For Sale: What You Should Watch Out for When Buying a Vizsla

It is necessary that you do your research if you plan on buying a Vizsla.

Below are questions you can ask your breeder:

- Ask the breeder for bloodline information and the coefficient of inbreeding (COI), as genetic problems are an issue, above a certain coefficient.
- Request to see both of the pups' parents, or at least, the litter's mother
- Find out hip and elbow scores for both parents. Though this is not a guarantee that the puppy will be exempted, it shows at least that the breeder has taken an effort to minimize risks.

If you want your Vizsla to participate in dog shows and other competitions, look for a show breeder who breeds pups to meet the standard appearance demanded in a dog show. You may also meet a performance breeder, who emphasizes an active temperament and sharp working drive for hunting. Research as much as possible about the questions you need to ask the breeder as well as questions you should expect the breeder to ask you.

Vizsla Rescue- Vizsla Puppies Rescue

What is Vizsla Rescue?

Some Vizslas are bought by people without a clear understanding and acceptance of the responsibility it demands. Other dogs become victims of abuse or unfortunate circumstances. They end up in the care of rescue groups, in need of rehabilitation, adoption, or fostering. If you plan to get an adult Vizsla, a rescue group or shelter is a good place to start. You need to keep in mind, however, that some rescue Vizslas will probably have health issues, and some of them do not have any prior training.

Rescue groups and shelters ensure that a dog's medical needs are addressed before it is transferred to its new family. All dogs are also spayed or neutered before adoption. You must also see that the animal shelter environment has quarantine protocols, as an extra precaution against illness or temperament problems.

How Can I Adopt a Rescue Vizsla?

Here is a step-by-step process for adopting a rescued Vizsla:

1. A prospective owner will be asked to fill out an adoption application to help match the best dog for a family.
2. The adopter will sign a contract to ensure he or she will be responsible for the care and well-being of the dog, to submit to follow-up visits, and to arrange obedience training as needed.
3. You must also pay a fee as required by the rescue group.

How do I surrender my Vizsla to rescue?

- Contact the closest State Rescue Coordinator for more information about placing a Vizsla to rescue.
- Prepare the necessary paperwork at the time of transfer. This includes registration papers, health records, and any other paperwork relating to the dog.
- See to it also that your dog is already neutered or spayed, and updated with shots as much as possible.

How much does a rescued Vizsla cost?

Each rescue organization sets its fees, but expect to pay a reasonable amount to cover expenses for procedures such as neutering or spaying, health exams by a licensed veterinarian, and microchipping.

Vizsla Adoption

Vizsla Puppies for Adoption

The foster family could tell you about the dog's behavior, as evaluated in a home setting.

The foster family has the closest experience with the dog and is the best source of information you can have about the dog's behavior, as evaluated in a home setting.

However, a disadvantage you might prepare for is that you cannot be sure if problematic genes are present in the dog, as dogs from rescue groups usually have an unknown background. Typically, it is more expensive to adopt a dog from a rescue group than from an animal shelter or humane society, but know that the dog has already been groomed, basic-trained, neutered, treated for any health problems, and socialized.

Adopting from an Animal Shelter

Shelter dogs cost much less than a dog from a good breeder. A purebred Vizsla from a breeder can cost around $1000 or more. This cost may not cover other expenses that your Vizsla needs, such as medical shots, and spaying or neutering. When you're adopting from a shelter, you would need to pay for the cost that was spent caring for the dog (including food and its stay in the shelter), and the necessary procedures to make the dog healthy and fit to live with you. If you add all the expenses that a shelter demands, they will still be much lower than getting a new puppy or adult dog from a breeder.

Adult Vizsla as an Instant Friend

You will need to set your expectations that the process of bonding with an adult Vizsla, as it will be different than with a puppy. Regardless of life stages, you need to spend enough time with your Vizsla to establish that bond. This is made easier thanks to the Vizsla's affectionate personality.

Adult Vizsla Adoption = Truly Saving a Life

It is a fact that shelters can get overpopulated with the dogs they rescue, or are surrendered to them. When there are too many animals that the shelter can care for, they sometimes have to resort to euthanasia to manage the population. Adoption can save a dog from this terrible fate.

What is a Pre-purchase/Adoption Test and How to Conduct It?

A pre-purchase/adoption test will help you evaluate yourself as an aspiring dog owner, as well as your preparedness and suitability with your new dog. This test will also guide you as you screen dogs that you will choose as your pet.

Below are tips for a quick test when deciding to buy or adopt a dog:

Ask Questions

- Why is the dog here? Know why the dog was turned over to the shelter.
- Does the dog have any medical issues?
- What's the best and worst thing about this dog?
- Has the dog been tested for temperament? Temperament tests try to gauge a dog's personality, but keep in mind that this is just a snapshot of a dog's personality at the moment of testing.

Assess the Dogs

If the shelter is unable to give you the information you need to know about the dog, spend some time observing it. See how it reacts to other people. If it does not respond, it may feel ill or was not socialized properly. If the dog is pacing and whining, it could be feeling uncomfortable and anxious. If the dog is isolating itself at the back of the kennel, it could be a sign of depression.

Walk up to the door of the kennel

Observe if the dog is showing signs of aggression or excitement. Signs of aggression may include growling, and the hair standing up on its back. If you see the dog wagging its tail, jumping around, and licking your hand, this is most likely a friendly dog that can be managed more easily.

Take the dog to a quiet room or yard

At this time, you are alone with the dog. Notice how it responds to you. This may give a different result from the previous step, as this allows you to be closer to the dog. Try to approach it, and drop any signs of nervousness or hostility. Allow the dog to feel comfortable in your presence.

Is it okay with a gentle pat?

It's a good sign if the dog is comfortable with this gesture. If it moves away, freezes, or growls, these may be signs of possible experiences that have negatively affected the dog.

Do a gut check

Doing the previous steps will give you an idea of how you feel about the dog. Often, your instincts will give you a sense of which particular dog is right for you.

Together with your research and conducting the test, you will be able to assess if the Vizsla you have found is a suitable pet for you.

CHAPTER 6

Essential Items for Your Vizsla

There are a few essential items you'll need to ensure your Vizsla has a healthy and happy experience living with you in your home.

Dog Food for Vizslas – Different Kinds and What Is the Best for Your Vizsla

One of the things you need to buy is, of course, dog food. One of the primary ingredients that you need to look out for is animal-based protein. Avoid grain and corn if you see this on the food list, as the Vizsla is prone to hyperthyroidism. Also, ensure that your dog always has access to clean water.

Vizslas are medium to large sized dogs; it would be best to buy dog food specific to their size. Moreover, you could also consult the dog breeder or a vet for your Vizsla's proper diet and the frequency of meals. Below is a list of top four high-quality dog foods for your Vizsla:

1. Annamaet Ultra Formula
2. Earthborn Holistic Primitive Natural

3. Merrick Grain-Free Real Texas Beef & Sweet Potato Dry Dog Food
4. New Formula* ACANA Grasslands Regional Formula Grain-Free Dry Dog Food

The Vizsla breed is affectionate. They always want to be around you!

Medium to large-sized dogs are prone to hip dysplasia. Considering this, you may think about buying dog food that is formulated with ingredients that address bone and joint problems.

Vizsla Dog Beds – Which Are the Best Types?

It is helpful to choose the right bed for your Vizsla, to make it feel comfortable. An important factor to consider is that the bed should be in proportion to your Vizsla's size.

Popular dog beds include the nest dog beds. These are oval-shaped or round with raised sides, which gives the feeling of being contained. Also, check for the material quality of the filling to ensure protection from hard surfaces.

With the Vizsla's short coat, it is also essential that the dog needs to be warm, especially during cold weather. The cave bed is a good option; this type of bed has a hood that gives more coverage for your dog.

Below is a list of appropriate dog beds to consider:

- Bagel Dog Bed for Nesters.
- Beasley's Dog Couch for Serious Snoozers.
- Ultimate Memory Foam Lounger.
- Serta Orthopedic Quilted Couch.
- XXL Overstuffed Orthopedic Dog Pillow.
- Orthopedic Memory Foam Joint Relief Bolster Bed.
- Big Barker Pillowtop Bolster Bed.
- Snoozer Cozy Dog Cave.

Vizsla Collar – How to Choose One?

Below are steps on how to measure your dog's neck, which you'll want to do before purchasing a collar.:

Step 1 – Measuring Your Dog's Head and Neck

Have your dog sit in front of you. With a piece of string or a soft tape measure, do the following:

- Head Size: The head's actual size is from the top of the dog's throat, over the ears up until the top of the head.
- Neck Size: See to it that you can slide two of your fingers between your dog's neck and the tape measure. Two fingers should make the collar size about 2 inches (5 centimeters) larger than the dog's neck size.

Step 2 – Choosing the Right-Sized Collar

Take the neck and head sizes from Step 1 for martingale type collars. Then, order a collar that will fall within this measurement range. If you order a martingale collar with a buckle, prepare the neck size.

For side-release buckle-type collars, take the neck size and see if it fits within one of the standard size ranges.

Vizsla Harnesses – What You Need to Look for When Buying One

Harnesses Can Keep Your Dog Healthy

If your dog constantly pulls on your leash while you walk, this may cause its windpipes to be slowly crushed. To avoid this, you may want to invest in a good quality dog harness. This is fastened around the dog's body and minimizes the pressure placed on the dog's neck and windpipe. To find the right size for your Vizsla, measure around the ribcage. You may buy one that has a few inches of allowance. Make sure it is not too tight that it will become uncomfortable for your dog, and not too loose that it can slide out of it.

Vizsla Muzzle – Does Your Dog Need One?

The muzzle is worn around your dog's mouth to restrain it from moving. There are certain situations when a muzzle must be used. It is important to understand why, when, and how to use a muzzle.

When Is a Dog Muzzle Needed?

- **Emergencies.** Your Vizsla may be injured, and further movements may cause the injury to worsen.
- **Your dog is observed to likely bite surrounding people/animals.** Your dog may have had a biting incident in the past, and it is essential to have the behavior addressed proactively by a behaviorist or trainer. Doing this can also prevent injuries that may be inflicted on other people and animals.
- **Grooming sessions.** Your Vizsla may not be accustomed to strangers grooming it. This may cause the dog to be hostile towards the groomer. You may consider putting the muzzle on your dog to ensure everyone's safety.
- **Breed specific legislation.** Some states or provinces have breed specific legislation (BSL) that requires a muzzle to be worn by certain so-called "dangerous breeds" in public. If you are traveling to these locations, be sure to do your research, and find out if your Vizsla needs to wear a muzzle in that particular area.

What Should I Not Use a Muzzle For?

It is not recommended that a dog muzzle be used for addressing behavioral problems, such as barking and chewing. If you do so, the dog will create a negative association with the muzzle and will feel anxious when it sees it. It is only meant to be used when it is needed, and only for a short period. Making your dog wear it for an extended period of time will inhibit panting, eating, and drinking.

Vizsla Toys

Vizsla Chew Toys

Dog toys can keep your Vizsla busy and out of trouble. Providing your Vizsla with toys can channel its chewing away from your shoes and other household items. This breed loves to chew, and will chew whatever is available unless it's provided with something specific to chew on.

The Vizsla loves to chew and will put its mouth on to anything unless it's provided with something for an outlet for this natural behavior.

Good chew toys for Vizslas are made of these three materials: nylon, rawhide, or hard rubber. The best of these are nylon, as it can be easily digested if swallowed. Rawhide, on the other hand, is good if the dog takes time to chew. This is not advisable for Vizslas, who immediately swallow things they chew on, as this can cause intestinal blockages. Chew toys made of rubber should be solidly built so it will not be easily torn apart. Avoid chew toys with plastic squeaks, which can be easily detached, and can cause choking.

Dog toy brands that are known for its durability are the Kong chew toys and the Nylabones. The Kong Company http://www.kongcompany.com offers a variety of dog toys that suit every dog's need and life stages.

The Nylabone company http://www.nylabone.com have non-edible and edible types of chew toys. The company also has a guide on how to choose the chew toy that best suits your dog.

Other Toys for Vizslas

Aside from chew toys, there are other items that can stimulate your Vizsla, and prevent it from getting bored. Pet companies have created puzzles where you can put treats inside, and the dog would need to solve it before a treat is dispensed.

CHAPTER 7
Vizslas And Your Home

Outdoors or indoors, the Vizsla can easily adapt to its surroundings. You need to provide it, however, with enough open space to allow it to run and exercise.

Vizslas are very hyper. They like to move around and play!

Don't let yours become lethargic!

How to Make Your Home Safe for Your Dog

Because of the lack of undercoat, Vizslas are sensitive to the cold weather. You will need to protect your dog from such weather conditions by providing its own place that is warm and dry. This is where a dog bed can come in useful.

Stow away any potentially hazardous items that your Vizsla may come across. These items include hanging wires and cables, children's toys, plants, heating, and air vents. Keep your valuable items inside cabinets or other storage spaces where your Vizsla cannot access it; you do not want to come home to find your expensive clothes and shoes chewed up.

As much as possible, keep your Vizsla from wandering into your bathroom, where it can potentially access bath and cleaning items, such as shampoos, chlorine, and bleaches. You may also consider installing baby gates to block off certain areas that you don't want your Vizsla to enter. If you have a backyard, this will become the exercise and training space for your Vizsla. Provide shelter for your dog, such as a dog house, so it can have a space to rest.

Vizslas and Space – How Much Does the Dog Need?

Vizslas are very hyper and have a lot of energy to expend. They like to move around and play. With these characteristics, space is a crucial thing to consider. A spacious lawn or backyard is ideal for your Vizsla. Place a fence to prevent your Vizsla from wandering out on the street.

If you live in an apartment, however, you can still provide the space it needs to stretch its muscles. Find access to an open field or running space to take your Vizsla by scouting for nearby parks. You can also take this time to explore outside with your dog.

How Can You Introduce Your Vizsla to Its New Home?

Introducing your new Vizsla to your home is important, as it may feel overwhelmed with the new surroundings. To do this, take your Vizsla on a long walk around your neighborhood, going to your house. This will drain the Vizsla's energy and will make it easier to manage once its inside. Let your Vizsla wear its collar and leash, and tour it around your house one room at a time. Do not allow it to wander on its own; this is also a good opportunity to assert your leadership by going in first and letting the dog follow you. Allow it to spend a few minutes inside each room while checking its behavior.

Make Gentle Introductions

If there are a number of family members living with you in your house, it's best to orient them to remain calm when you introduce your Vizsla. It may be tempting for them to rush to your new dog, and start cuddling it.

Meeting the Family

Start by introducing your Vizsla to the adults. Observe how it responds to them, and let it take some time to get acquainted with each family member. If everything goes well, you can proceed with the children. Kids can get excited, and may start to grab your dog. Instruct your kids to gently pat and hold your Vizsla.

The Vizsla is moderately patient and is tolerant with infants, but it is best never to assume this is true all the time. To introduce your infant to the dog, let someone hold the baby, and allow the Vizsla to come near slowly. Always supervise the interaction between your baby and your Vizsla.

Owning a Vizsla is a big responsibility and commitment. Ask your family members to pitch in to make living with your new dog easier. Designate tasks to family members in taking care of the dog. Decide who will be the overall head or caretaker. One may be tasked with feeding, while the other's responsibility is grooming the dog. Be clear about the rules and routine the dog

has to follow, and be consistent to train it effectively.

How Should You House Train Your Vizsla?

A Vizsla has a short attention span and might get bored quickly during training sessions, especially when they are still young.

The Vizsla's intelligence will give you a good start in training. You need to channel this intelligence efficiently; otherwise, they can get easily bored and uninterested. When they are younger, these dogs have shorter attention spans, so you need to keep them constantly focused when training.

Some essential skills your dog can master are crate training, bladder, and bowel control. (Refer back to Chapter 3, for more information).

Use positive reinforcement while housebreaking puppies or adult dogs. If you catch it pooping or urinating in an inappropriate place, give commands such as 'freeze' or 'no,' to startle it enough to stop, and give you time to lead it to its potty spot. If you live in a high-rise building, try litter pan training. Get a pan that is proportional to your Viszla's size, and train it to relieve itself in the pan.

Dogs mark their territory by urinating in certain spots. You will need to correct this behavior by consulting a dog trainer. To remove the scent, spray deodorizers on the places where your Vizsla has marked.

It takes patience to house train your Vizsla, and this may go on for weeks to months.

What are the Possible Hazards in Your House That

Can Harm Your Vizsla?

There are everyday items in your house that can potentially harm your Vizsla. These include garbage, cleaning materials, broken glass, hanging wires and cables, and batteries. Another thing pet owners overlook is the effect of airborne toxins on pets. Secondhand smoke, bleach vapors, and paint fumes pose damaging risks to pets, too. Construction dust, insulation particles, asbestos or mold, which are common side effects of any renovation project, are also unsafe.

Ways to Keep Your House Vizsla-safe

- Keep garbage bins tightly covered.
- Do not put expired medicine in the trash or down the drain.
- Keep your Vizsla away during cleaning and renovation activities.
- Keep hazardous items out of reach for pets (tables, counters, etc.)
- Lock up cleaning supplies and renovation materials in a cabinet.

Refer back to the section "How to Make Your Home Safe For Your Dog" of this chapter for more information.

Immediately see a veterinarian if you suspect your Vizsla has ingested or inhaled toxins.

How Should You Introduce Your Vizsla to Other Pets?

If you have other pets in your house that are still young and small, be extra careful when introducing your Vizsla to them. Their hunting instincts may drive them to think that the baby animals are prey.

Vizslas get along well with most cats. To introduce them to each other, provide your cat with a tall and stable shelf where it can retreat, should your Vizsla get excited. Remember also not to force them to interact, as this may cause traumatic consequences for both of the animals.

If you have another dog, a smooth introduction is also possible if you walk your Vizsla together with it. This will give them time to get acquainted with each other. It is also better if you have one person walk the other dog. Stay apart at first, then move together slowly towards each other, side by side. Do this until you see they become at ease with each other. If all goes well for a time, you can now try an off-leash play in neutral territory.

How Can You Spend Time With Your Vizsla?

The Vizsla can be your companion in a variety of activities: hunting, jogging, trailing, and trekking. That is why an owner with an active lifestyle can be a good fit for the Vizsla; you will be able to do things together that are interesting for both of you. The Vizsla can also be content lounging with you in your bed, or on your lap on lazy days.

Training your Vizsla for dog sports and competitions is also another good way to spend time with it.

Vizslas may see children as their competition for your affection. Kids must be taught how to interact with the Vizsla. They may see puppies as toys and may handle them harshly. When your dog is interacting with children, proper supervision is important.

Families with children also need to think about the time and energy their pet Vizsla needs. It will be a challenge housetraining a pup while toilet training a human at the same time. In most cases, the pup usually ends up compromised.

CHAPTER 8

How to Groom Your Vizsla

Vizslas are low maintenance dogs that are easy to clean. This breed has very little odor compared to most dogs. The Vizsla is the ideal pet for those with a sensitive nose, and those who do not have the time to bathe their dog every week. They also shed fur minimally.

The Vizsla Coat – What Do You Need to Know About It?

The Vizsla lacks an undercoat (fluffy and short hair lying close

to the body). These dogs have a short, easy-to-care-for coat that requires only occasional brushing. To freshen the coat, you can wipe its fur with a damp towel, or use a dry dog shampoo.

The Vizsla is the ideal pet for those with a sensitive nose, and those who do not have the time to bathe their dog every week.

Vizsla Shedding – Is It a Concern?

Vizslas are low shedders, and when they do shed, their fur will not be clearly seen because it is so short. You can use a non-cotton sweater to pick up the loose hairs.

Diet or skin problems can also influence shedding. This is evident when the coat is dry or lacks shine.

Regularly brushing the Vizsla's fur helps reduce the amount of loose hair, and evenly distributes its coat oils. This can keep it looking shiny and healthy. Weekly, you can minimize their shedding using a rubber bristle brush to remove loose hair.

Vizsla Shampoo – How to Choose the Best One

It is not necessary to bathe your Vizsla frequently. You can even give your Vizsla a full bath once every three months. To keep it clean, you only need to wipe its body with a damp towel regularly.

If your Vizsla has allergies or sensitive skin, consider using a hypoallergenic shampoo, and follow it with a medicated shampoo depending on its needs. If your Vizsla has normal skin, you can include the second bath with a fragrant conditioner that is fortified with vitamins B and E. This can reduce the amount of hair your dog will shed and can give the coat a bright shine. To control flaking and dandruff (especially in dry conditions), you can use a hydrating spray in between baths.

Below are the steps for bathing your Vizsla:

1. Brush its fur to remove dead hair and mats.
2. If you are using a tub, place a rubber mat inside to keep the dog from slipping. Fill the tub with three to four inches of lukewarm water.
3. Use a spray hose, pitcher, or a plastic cup to wet the dog. Be careful with the eyes, ears, and nose.
4. Gradually squeeze the pet shampoo on its body and work on

a lather, saving the head for last.

5. Rinse thoroughly. Start with the head to prevent soap from dripping into the eyes.

6. Towel dry.

Vizsla Brush

What Are the Different Types of Vizsla Brushes?

Dogs with short, smooth coats, such as the Vizsla breed, can be easily maintained.

Dogs with short, smooth coats like the Vizsla are low maintenance in the area of grooming. Although this breed does not require much grooming, they need a nice, weekly brushing using a bristle brush. It also makes way for good blood flow. It removes loose hair, spreads natural oils, and keeps the skin healthy. Start brushing from front to back, working throughout the skin. You can also use a dry towel to wipe its coat.

What Is the Best Brush for Your Vizsla?

The suggested brush for your Vizsla is a slicker, bristle, or steel pin brush.

How to Take Care of Your Vizsla's Nails

You may want to take your Vizsla out for a walk before clipping its nails. Doing so can lower its energy, so it won't struggle against you when you're starting the task.

Prepare treats and give positive reinforcement to associate nail clipping with a positive experience. As you start to clip, gently press on your dog's paws to help it become familiar with the feeling of clipping its nails. Then, work gradually, trimming down a thin portion of the nail at first, making sure you do not reach the quick (the pink area inside the nail that contains nerves and blood vessels). After clipping one nail, reward your dog with a treat. As you proceed, increase the number of nails you clip in one sitting to help your dog get used to the process. Never trim extremely long nails short in one sitting, as you might accidentally clip the dog's quick. Instead, work gradually, shaving small portions of your dog's nails off each time.

You will know if you are getting closer to the quick if the nail is getting softer. You must always remember to avoid clipping the quick; doing so will cause it to bleed, cause much pain, and may lead to infections.

How to Clean Your Vizsla's Ears

It is always important to routinely check and clean your dog's ears. This way, you will be aware of any infections that are starting to spread.

To do this, you will need cotton balls, and oil (you may use mineral, olive, or witch hazel). Moisten the cotton ball with the oil, and gently wipe it in your dog's ear. Be careful to avoid the ear canal. Using a Q-tip is highly discouraged, as it may damage the inner ear if your dog suddenly moves or jerks its head.

CHAPTER 9

Healthcare and Maintenance for Your Vizsla

Vizslas are an active breed and need at least 60 minutes of exercise every day. They enjoy long walks, jogging, playing fetch, and other outdoor exercises.

Vizsla Health: Things You Need to Know About

The Vizsla is a vigorous dog breed with good stamina. This fuels them to endure outdoor activities such as tracking, pointing, and retrieving.

What Are Common Vizsla Health Problems?

Just like any breed, Vizslas are also prone to certain diseases.

Vizslas can suffer from separation anxiety, which can lead to destructive behaviors.

Below are the common health problems of Vizslas

- Cancer (especially lymphosarcoma and hemangiosarcoma)
- Hip dysplasia (7% out of the 15,000 X-rays of Vizslas were found dysplastic, as the evaluation of the Orthopedic Foundation of America.) This causes pain and lameness, and can require expensive surgery. Elbow dysplasia and osteochondritis occur less frequently.
- Hereditary eye diseases in Vizslas can lead to blindness. These are progressive retinal atrophy (PRA), eyelid abnormalities (entropion and ectropion), cataracts, and glaucoma. These eye problems include allergies, which can also cause the skin to itch.
- Hypothyroidism
- Gastrointestinal syndrome or "bloat" (occurs mostly to all deep-chested breeds with a higher-than-normal risk).

- Skin diseases, which include sebaceous adenitis, and demodectic mange.
- Blood-clotting diseases, such as von Willebrand's disease, and hemophilia.

Preventing health problems

Ensure your Vizsla is updated with vaccinations, and take it to your vet regularly for a check-up.

Feed it with high-quality dog food that has animal-based protein as one of the primary ingredients. Some vitamins and supplements you can give your Vizsla include Probiotic and Digestive Support, Natural Joint Support, and Fish Oil.

Vizsla Weight- How to Maintain Your Dog's Healthy Weight Range?

The weight range for male Vizslas is around 45 to 65 pounds (20 to 29 kilograms), with females weighing less.

A young Vizsla (about 4 to 12 months) requires around 1114 kilocalories per day. Choose a puppy food appropriate for medium to large-sized breeds. It is recommended that this food is given to your puppy when it has reached 10 to 12 months old, or when it reaches about 90% of his adult size. Young Vizslas need to be fed 3 to 4 meals a day, while an adult Vizsla needs to have 2 meals a day. An active adult Vizsla weighing 55 pounds needs an average daily intake of 1409 kilocalories.

There are some ways you can initially assess your Vizsla's weight. Do the eye and hands-on test: first, look at its body, focusing on the waist. Second, place your hands on its back, with thumbs along the spine, with the fingers spread downward. You should be able to feel its ribs without having to press hard. If you can't, it needs less food and more exercise. Always confirm your observations with your veterinarian, before minimizing your Vizsla's food portions.

Which Vizsla Vaccinations Are Recommended?

It is mandatory that you take your Vizsla to the vet every year for its booster shots. The right vaccinations will help protect your dog's health, but not all vaccinations are necessary. Essential shots include Parvovirus, Distemper, and Rabies.

Do not give vaccinations to puppies under four weeks. The mother's milk can provide all the nutrients the puppy needs for protection against illnesses, during this period.

Your Vizsla should receive vaccinations and preventive injections for the following:

- Distemper
- Hepatitis
- Leptospirosis
- Parvovirus KF-11
- Parainfluenza/Bordetella
- Coronavirus
- Wormer
- Rabies

Puppy's Age	Recommended Vaccinations	Optional Vaccinations
6 to 8 weeks	DHPP	Bordetella
10 to 12 weeks	DHPP (vaccines for distemper, adenovirus [hepatitis], parainfluenza, and parvovirus)	Coronavirus, Leptospirosis, Bordetella, Lyme disease
Every six months	Bordetella (Kennel Cough- required for boarding facilities)	
14 to 16 weeks	DHPP, Rabies	Coronavirus, Lyme disease, Leptospirosis
12 to 16 months	DHPP, Rabies	Coronavirus, Leptospirosis, Bordetella, Lyme disease
Every year	Leptospirosis, Lyme disease	Coronavirus, Bordetella
Every three years	Rabies (as required by law), DHPP	None

What Are the Vizsla's Nutritional Requirements?

According to the National Research Council of the National Academies, an active adult Vizsla weighing 55 pounds

(25 kilograms) requires a daily caloric intake of 1,409 kilocalories on average. Dogs that are older, or have been spayed or neutered, may need fewer calories. If you go to the field and work with your Vizsla, it will need 1,565 kilocalories a day. Growing puppies eat more than adults. A young Vizsla puppy (6 to 12 months) weighing 35 pounds (16 kilograms) needs an estimated 1,115 kilocalories per day. Always check if you need to adjust your dog's food intake, based on its activity level and other factors.

When buying adult dog food for your Vizsla, ideal ingredients to look out for are glucosamine, chondroitin, green-lipped mussels, SAM-e, and MSM. You can also buy some of these supplements separately; ask your vet which are suitable for your Vizsla.

How Can You Prevent or Control Your Vizsla's Internal Parasites, Fleas and Ticks?

Daily inspections of your Vizsla for ticks and fleas during the warm seasons, are critical.

It is crucial to check your Vizsla for ticks and fleas daily, especially during the warm seasons.

Ticks are parasites that can survive for years. They wait for a host to pass by, and leap onto it. Then, they attach to the host within a few hours. They then dig their head into the skin and sucks the host's blood. They drop off the host to lay thousands of eggs. The worst thing about ticks is that they can transmit diseases. These include Lyme disease, Rocky Mountain spotted fever, and tick paralysis.

Examine your dog each time you return from a walk in the woods or field. Although they can clamp on anywhere, ticks like to place themselves between the toes and around the dog's ears.

How to Prevent Ticks and Fleas

Run a wide-tooth comb on your dog after a walk. There is a chance you'll find ticks on your dog's coat, which has not yet latched on to its skin. Mowing tall grasses will also do well, to avoid ticks setting up camp.

Treatments to Keep Your Dog Tick-free

- **Topical treatments.** Active ingredients that make it effective include permethrin, imidacloprid, pyrethrin, or fipronil. Apply a small amount of the solution to the dog's back.
- **Sprays.** These require you to cover all areas of the dog's body; be careful around eyes and ears, and be sure to spray in a well-ventilated area. Active ingredients include pyrethrin or permethrin.

- **Powders.** These can relieve itching and can repel ticks. Read the directions, and how long the effects should last. These contain pyrethrin.
- **Shampoos and dips.** These are used for dogs already infested with ticks. Work on a good lather around your dog's body and leave it on for 10 minutes before washing it off.
- **Collars.** Tick collars work in two ways: one, by repelling pests through emitting certain active ingredients that can kill ticks on contact, and two, when the dog absorbs the medication in its fat layer, where the tick can be killed once it bites your dog's skin. These typically contain carbamates and pyrethroids. Its effect may wear off when it is wet, so it may not be ideal if your Vizsla spends some time in the water. Read directions carefully to see how long the collar remains active, and choose one that snugly fits your Vizsla's neck.

When It's Time to See a Vet

When the tick infestation becomes severe, this might require stronger treatments to eradicate it fully. Signs telling you it's time to see your vet include: one or more ticks can be seen deep in the ear canal, redness or swelling at the site of the tick bite that lasts beyond two or three days after removal, and changes in your dog's behavior or health after a tick bite.

How Can You Properly Exercise Your Vizsla?

An adult Vizsla will need daily long, brisk walks. A game of fetch in the park or in your yard will also work well. You may also allow it to run around your yard, with the same amount of time that it needs to get its full exercise. As this breed is high-energy, not giving them enough exercise will make them bored and destructive.

You can set up an obstacle course in your yard for your dog to tackle. This can provide an outlet for exercise and stimulation for its brain.

A young Vizsla (18 months or younger), will need restricted exercise – 20-minute walks, fetch games or playing with other dogs. Running, and long-distance treks, should not be forced.

How Can You Take Care of Your Vizsla When It Gets Older?

Your Vizsla will be more prone to diseases as it ages. As a Vizsla grows older, its elbows and hips may become stiff. This can be a risk for dysplasia, an inherited disease that causes the joints to develop improperly, and results in arthritis. You may also notice that it has difficulty getting up.

When you see signs of dysplasia, it's better to take it for an X-ray to identify issues as early as possible. Surgery can be a good choice if it is already at a critical and life-limiting stage.

Sometimes your Vizsla's kneecap (patella) may slip out of place (called patellar luxation). You might also notice when your Vizsla runs, it suddenly skips or hops for a few strides, then kicks its leg out to the sides to pop the kneecap back in place. If this is the case for one leg, it will not require much more treatment than the medication for arthritis. When symptoms are getting severe, surgery may be needed to realign the kneecap to keep it from popping out of place.

Keep your Vizsla healthy by providing it with food rich in nutrients, and in portions that will not allow it to become overweight. Do not let your Vizsla struggle with obesity when it gets old. Being overweight puts a huge strain on the joints.

CHAPTER 10

Vizsla Breeding

Different Vizsla Breeders

Wirehaired Vizsla Breeders

A reputable Wirehaired Vizsla breeder will have and do:

- A membership of recognized dog clubs.
- Researched pedigrees (to better understand and reduce health risks).
- Does not sell breeding pairs.
- Willing to discuss the positive and negative aspects of the breed.
- Evaluate each puppy's characteristics to try to match the right puppy to you.

Below are things you need to clarify and confirm:

- **Pedigree.** The breeder should be able to provide pedigree information of the father (sire) and the mother (dam).
- **Health Clearances.** The breeder should be able to provide you with information on the health test results for the puppy's parents.

- **Test or Show Results.** The breeder should provide proof of the accomplishments, and show results.

A reputable Vizsla breeder's contact with you does not stop after the purchase is complete!

Good Vizsla Breeders – How to Find and Recognize One

It is always best to buy your puppy from a reputable and responsible breeder. You may be enticed with fancy websites – breeders willing to sell you a puppy after completing the online application and paying through online payment portals, such as Paypal; other websites selling puppies may say they accept credit card payments. Remember that reputable breeders will want to see you before they sell you their puppies. If a website shows the breeder having several litters per year, or says, "Puppies always available" or "Large selection available," choose another breeder.

When you purchase from a responsible breeder, you can be confident that the puppy has been given proper treatment, which includes insurance of correct and typical temperament, good health, and conformation.

Below is a list of questions you should ask the breeder, with answers you should expect them to provide.

Q: Where do the puppies live?

A: "In the house with the family." A puppy that's born into family life is probably more socialized and relaxed, while a puppy that grew up isolated (in a garage or backyard) and away from humans tends to be either aggressive or shy.

Q: Can I meet the parents?

A: Meeting the father may not be possible, but you should certainly meet the mother. The puppy's parents will give you a preview of its temperament and personality.

Q: In a year, how many litters do you raise?

A: A good breeder will only have one litter a year. This will give ample time to take care of them and provide them with the handling they need. Each female dog should be bred no more than once a year.

Q: Can I have copies of the health clearances?

A: The breeder should present health clearances–documentation from an independent agency, such as the Orthopedic Foundation for Animals, or the Canine Eye Registration Foundation – showing that the parent and grandparent dogs were tested for hereditary problems. Since some genetic conditions are not yet evident until adulthood, health clearances aren't available for dogs less than two years old. With that, a responsible breeder won't breed dogs until they're two or three years old.

A reputable breeder's contact with you does not stop after the purchase is complete. They will follow-up with you to check the puppy's condition, answer your questions, and suggest things you can do to keep your puppy healthy.

Even though you might find a puppy priced much lower elsewhere, you might end up paying for a lot of other expenses, if you do not purchase from a reputable breeder.

Here are some tips to help you find a reputable and responsible breeder:

- You can check and contact local Vizsla Clubs in your area to see if they have breeder listings or breeder referral program.
- Attend a show and purchase a show catalog. It is better to talk to an exhibitor after the show.
- Try to contact other Vizsla owners and enthusiasts online. They may be able to give you information on where to find responsible breeders.

Signs of a reputable breeder:

- They keep the place clean. The dog's area is sanitary, safe, and well-supplied with fresh water, toys, and beds. If there is a toilet area in the puppy's quarters, this means that the puppies have already begun house training.

- The breeder asks you to sign a neuter/spay contract, promising to spay/neuter your pup, if you're buying a dog who's not going to be bred.
- The breeder does not advertise or specialize variations in sizes, or colors that are unusual for the breed. Extremely small or huge dogs are prone to health problems. Also, trying to breed for other colors or sizes is a sign that the breeder is more interested in making money than breeding healthy puppies.
- The breeder should take the dog back, at any stage of the dog's life, if in case you're unable to take care of the dog anymore. A good breeder will insist on doing this.
- The breeder won't let you take the puppy home before it is eight weeks old.

Bad Vizsla Breeders – The Telltale Signs

You need to educate yourself to spot signs of bad Vizsla breeders. Some breeders are just "backyard breeders" who have little experience or knowledge breeding Vizslas.

- They breed dogs without considering and taking the time to make good genetic matches or registering their dogs with the right kennel or breed club.
- Some breeders let their dogs breed without researching their family history in terms of health and behavior. They do not consider investigating possible genetic health issues in both the parents and the puppies. They may charge a lower price for the puppies, as compared to a responsible breeder, but this may leave you to pay more for the dogs when health issues arise.

- In many cases, these breeders will not take the puppies back if something goes wrong.

If you do not mind owning a dog with an unknown genetic history, it is best to go to your local rescue group or shelter, where the puppies have been checked by the vet.

How to Avoid Bad Dog Breeders

As you look for a dog breeder, it is important to check references - find time to talk to other families that have bought a dog from that breeder. Search for other options until you are confident that you have found a responsible breeder.

Questions to Ask the Dog Breeder

- What type of care should I give to this breed? Does the breed have specific needs I should be aware of?
- How long have you been breeding dogs? How long have you produced this specific dog breed? Ideally, the breeder should have been doing it for several years already.
- Do you sell your dogs to pet stores, puppy brokers, wholesalers, or online? Responsible breeders do not sell their puppies in those outlets.
- Can I visit the facilities where you breed and house your dogs?
- Can I meet the litter of puppies and their mother?
- What is the health and behavior history of this puppy?
- What medical tests do the puppies get before selling them? Do you test the adult dogs before breeding? Find out what tests (OFA, CERT, etc.) are recommended by the national

breed club. If this breeder has not tested the dogs, then you should look for another breeder.

- Can I see the breed registration papers for the puppies and their parents?
- Can I see the veterinary records of the puppies and their parents?
- What happens if my dog is diagnosed with a hereditary disease? Is there a guarantee for the puppy I buy? The answer should be that the breeder will take the dog back, and refund all or part of what you paid for the dog, or work with you to treat the dog.
- Can you provide references from owners of the puppies from previous litters? (If no, ask why not. The breeder should always have references.)

Bad Breeder Warning Signs

If the breeder was able to answer all the questions above, appropriately, there are still things you need to be on the lookout for, including:

- Dogs in the facility appear to be in poor health.
- They breed two or more breeds or breed unrecognized varieties. The dogs have no titles, either working, sports, or showing. This means the breeder does not seek to improve the overall conformation of the breed. Breeding solely for "pet quality" means breeding for profit only, rather than for the betterment of the breed.
- They always have puppies for sale, sometimes two or three litters at a time.

- The breeder does not ask you anything about your house, and if the lifestyle you have suits the dog.
- The breeder is ready to sell the puppies even if they are still under eight weeks of age.
- Breeders advertise "rare" colors, sizes, or other traits (such as "rare" white Dobermans, or Great Danes, "king-sized" German Shepherds, etc.). These traits are most of the time the result of not following breed standards, and can lead to health or behavioral problems.
- They advertise or sell their puppies for greatly reduced prices.
- Breeds dogs under two years of age.

Puppy Mills

Most pet stores deal with large numbers of different breeds and have gotten them from puppy mills. These operations breed only for quantity, not quality. They have just one purpose: to make money. They rarely conduct health checks for their animals. The puppies from these places are not properly socialized, (which is very important for Vizslas), wormed or vaccinated. They do not pay attention to the breed standard or temperament, and the adult dogs are kept in filthy conditions.

What is the Best Time to Have Your Vizsla Mate for Breeding?

As you consider breeding your male or female Vizsla, here is a guide to questions you need to ponder beforehand:

- Why do you want to have a litter of puppies?
- In the event of a large litter (they can be above 12 puppies),

are you willing to keep them for around 7 to 8 months, and until they can be given to their new families?

- Will you be patient in getting to know more about a prospective owner? Are you prepared to refuse people, if you think the Vizsla isn't for them?
- Are you willing and able to take back the puppies if the owner can no longer take care of them?
- Are you willing to spend a lot of money to care for a litter of puppies? Pregnancy and delivery complications can be very costly.
- If your female Vizsla cannot feed the puppies, will you be prepared to feed them when needed?
- If you own the male, are you willing to let the female stay while the breeding takes place? This usually takes a minimum of two weeks. Can you ensure her safety at that time? What if she is unwilling to be bred? You must know how to respond to these situations, as it can also be potentially dangerous for your male Vizsla.

If you are still interested in breeding, also check the following items. These are things you need to consider, to find out if your dog is ready to breed.

Temperament

- What is your dog's personality? Is he/she great with your family? What about with strangers? Is your Vizsla hyper around new people? If your answer is yes, you need to consider if you want to pass on this trait to its puppies.

- Has it ever bitten or snapped at someone?
- Is your Vizsla aggressive towards other dogs?
- How trainable is your dog? Does it seem willing to learn new things?

Health

- Is your dog healthy? Does it have allergies or immune system problems?
- Have you taken it for hip and elbow X-rays? Have you tested it for CERF, thyroid problems, and von Willebrand disease?
- Are your dog's littermates healthy? If your dog has OFA certification on the status of its hips, but the rest of the litter is dysplastic, you probably should not consider breeding.

Conformation

- Does your dog conform to the AKC standard for Vizslas? Does it have any disqualifying traits?
- What are the characteristics and traits you have observed in your dog? Is it cow-hocked? Does it toe in or out? Does it lack depth of chest? Are its eyes light?
- Does your dog move correctly?

Connect with owners in your local Vizsla club, and learn more from people who are familiar with the AKC standards, to be well versed in this information.

Functionality

Is your dog able to do what it was bred for? The Vizsla was bred for hunting, and you should be able to see this trait and maintain the same for the puppies you wish to produce.

Titles

Titles do not ensure a dog's worthiness for breeding. Instead, they are a testament to your dog's conformation.

If you have firmly decided you want to breed your dog, you must start looking for a mate.

If you have a male, take him out where he can be seen, like joining your local Vizsla club, running, and hunting groups.

If you want to breed your female, it is important that she will be mated with the stud dog at the right time. She can only be mated when she is in season. Make sure you have already checked with the stud dog beforehand, negotiated with the owner, and other things you need to check and settle.

Consider your Vizsla's characteristics in all areas (temperament, health, conformation, and functionality), and look for a mate that develops strengths, and improves on the weaknesses.

Frequency of Season

A dog comes into 'season' or 'heat' (as it is often termed) twice a year. The female Vizsla's first season comes when she has become sexually mature, and this usually happens when she turns one year old. The frequency your Vizsla will be in heat will vary. The average season is every six months, while some will vary from every five to ten months.

Signs your female is in heat

The following symptoms may start to surface, signaling your female Vizsla is in season:

- The vulva starts to swell, and you find your dog frequently licking it.
- Blood spots appearing around the vulva.
- Urinating more frequently than usual.
- Loss of appetite.

When you start spotting blood, note the date, and make a call to the stud dog owner to make the arrangements.

Knowing the right time for mating

The heat or season has two stages: The first one is "pre-estrus," and the second is the "estrus." The duration of each stage depends on the breed, but on average, each stage will last 8 to 10 days.

Stage 1 – Pre-Estrus

This is when the dog has blood discharges and has an enlarged vulva. She is likely to reject advances from a stud dog at this stage.

Stage 2 – Estrus

In the second stage, the vulva will swell more, and the discharge becomes yellow. This is the time for the stud dog mating to be arranged. The most fertile time is approximately two days into the second stage, as this is when she is ovulating.

Many stud dog owners will allow two matings- two days straight, or two days apart. If you are unsure of the right time, however, you can ask your vet to do an ovulation test.

What Are Other Hungarian Dog Breeds You Can Pair With Your Vizsla?

Hungarian dog breeds include flock guards and herding dog breeds.

Here are other Hungarian dog breeds, which include flock guards and herding breeds.

1. **Kuvasz, Kuvaszok (plural of Kuvasz).** Brilliant, but are not that trainable. They are very independent-minded.

2. **Hungarian Greyhound.** They are excellent on the racetrack. They are tough, strong, and fast. It is sensible, intelligent, and loyal. They make a terrific companion and watchdog.
3. **Mudi.** An all-around working dog breed for herding, ratting and hunting small game. It is admired for its many different talents, and good disposition.
4. **Puli.** A small-medium flock guardian breed with a densely corded coat, similar to the Komondor, but usually black instead of white. The dogs used to be shorn together with the sheep to keep them cool during the hot summers. It is self-confident and intelligent.
5. **Pumi.** A medium-sized terrier-type breed of sheepdog that has a lot of energy. It has the intelligence of a herding dog along with the terrier's alertness.
6. **Transylvanian Hound.** Loyal and friendly, good-natured and well-mannered

The Pregnant Vizsla: How Should You Take Care of Her?

Upon finding out your dog is pregnant, there are some things you need to ensure she has a good experience.

Proper Nutrition

If your dog is already the right weight, and eating good quality dog food, you do not have to change her diet for the first part of her pregnancy (unless your veterinarian gives specific instructions to the contrary). As she gains weight during the last five weeks of her pregnancy, a gradual increase in food intake is recommended, until she consumes 35 to 50 percent more than usual. Slowly increase her food portions in small, frequent meals. Abruptly introducing large meals can cause discomfort. Remember to have water available at all times. Check with your vet if your Vizsla needs any prescribed nutritional supplements.

Workout Routine

Your pregnant dog needs to stay strong throughout the pregnancy. Continue to take her for walks, although these should be shorter, and done in safer places. Keep her away from the dog park, or areas where a lot of animals can surround her. Doing so can protect her from getting hurt by other aggressive dogs, or contracting any infections which could harm her babies.

Vet Visits: Having an Ally

Vet visits should include prenatal care, shots, heartworm blood test, and X-ray testing for hip dysplasia before mating. Regular visits to the vet are essential to keep your dog healthy during her pregnancy. Your vet will also examine your dog for signs of illness and discomfort.

It is always better to be prepared for an emergency. While you are at your vet for a prenatal checkup, also ask about what to do in case of an emergency, so you are prepared in case this happens.

How Can You Assist Your Vizsla When It Is Giving Birth?

The best thing to do is to set up a whelping box. It will give a more secure, warm, comfortable, and easy-to-clean location for your dog to deliver her puppies. Place it in a quiet area, away from all other dogs to give the mother privacy and safety.

Allow some time for your pregnant dog to be familiar with it. Dogs look for warm and safe places to deliver their puppies. Make sure you introduce her to the whelping box beforehand, so she won't deliver the puppies elsewhere.

Whelping supplies checklist:

- Thermometer, to check your dog's temperature.
- Newspaper, to cover the whelping box floor for easy cleanup.
- Tissue paper, to help with clean up.
- Anti-slip bath mats, to use for bedding after whelping is done.
- Dry, clean towels, to clean the puppies.
- Unwaxed dental floss, to tie off the umbilical cords.
- Clean scissors, to cut the umbilical cords.
- Iodine, to clean the puppies' abdomens after the cord is cut.
- Your veterinarian's phone number, and the number of the nearest pet clinic.

Keep these supplies in a clean location, and where they are easy to find.

Labor signs include:

- Your pregnant dog may stop eating a few days before whelping.
- Your Vizsla starts to pant heavily.
- Her temperature drops down, from 102.5° to 99° Fahrenheit, or even lower (39° to 37° Celsius). Approximately 24 hours after this temperature drop, she will whelp.

Whelping

Dogs are capable of giving birth on their own. Driven by instincts, she should know what to do. She may need assistance, especially when complications occur. If this is the case, be ready and on standby.

Each puppy is born enclosed by its placental membrane. Most of the time, the mother tears this membrane off or eats it. If she does not, you will have to remove it. Puppies cannot survive for more than a few minutes when their oxygen supply runs out.

The umbilical cord should also be severed as she cleans her pups. If she does not, assist her in snipping the cord, and tying it off with some unwaxed dental floss.

You should wipe the abdomen of all of the puppies using iodine to prevent infections from entering through the umbilical cord. The cord should be tied and cut about 1 to 2 inches (2.5 to 5 centimeters) from the puppy.

Keep track of the number of placentas. Remaining placentas can cause problems for the mother.

Keep an eye on the pups to make sure they are all breathing normally and nursing.

The puppies need warmth at all times. The ideal temperature is 75° Fahrenheit (24° Celsius). Bring a lamp and place it near the box with dim lights. You may also need blankets and towels to keep the area clean.

Possible Whelping Complications

Things may go wrong when your Vizsla delivers her puppies. It is crucial for owners to know what the warning signs are of labor complications.

Situations when you need to call your vet immediately include:

- If your dog seems to be in severe discomfort.
- If two or more hours have passed in between the delivery of puppies, or if your dog experiences strong contractions that last more than 45 minutes without birth.
- Shivering, trembling, and collapsing are warning signs of serious complications that could put both the mother and the puppies at risk.
- It is normal for dogs to discharge a dark green or bloody fluid following the first puppy. This is alarming, however, if it happens before the first puppy is out.
- If your dog shows no signs of whelping 64 days after her last mating.

Vizsla Puppies: How Do You Take Care of Newborn Puppies?

Newborn Puppy Nutrition

In the first few weeks of their lives, newborn puppies greatly depend on their mother for nutrition. During the first week, the mother produces colostrum, a milk-like substance that contains the essential maternal antibodies that the puppies will need as their immune systems develop. These antibodies help them fight off infections, and so it is crucial that all of the puppies receive enough colostrum at this time.

The American Kennel Club (AKC) advises that owners take note of the puppies' weight as they grow, especially during the first few weeks. Consult your vet about how much weight you should expect for your dog's breed, and check on all of the puppies, for signs of malnourishment.

Newborn Puppy Temperature Control

Newborn puppies need constant warmth, as they are very vulnerable to health issues when they are exposed to icy temperatures. Owners should make sure the new litter is kept warm in a safe and clean environment. It is highly recommended that owners place a heat lamp on the corner of the whelping box, in a slightly cooler area to give the puppies the right temperature. Putting it in the corner of the box allows the puppies to crawl to the other side if it's too warm. Position the lamp far enough that it does not burn the puppies and the mother. Heat lamps are the better option than heat pads; as heat pads are more likely to burn.

Feeding the Nursing Dog

When your Vizsla has finished delivering all the puppies, it may not eat within the first 24 hours. Continue to observe the mom and the newborn litter, and call your veterinarian if she still does not consume any food. This may indicate a post-natal complication.

Owners need to ensure the health of the mother since the puppies depend on her for their nutrition. Nursing dogs need more energy than pregnant or non-lactating dogs, especially as the puppies get older. You may need to change your dog's diet with a higher fat content while she is nursing. Ask your veterinarian for nutritional information during this time, and to help you find the right food for your nursing female.

One thing owners also need to be aware of are signs of canine mastitis – a bacterial infection of one or more of the lactating glands in the breast. A mother with mastitis will develop hot, dark, red, and painful teats. This causes discomfort for the mother, and she may snap at puppies who attempt to nurse. Mastitis can be caused by a scratch (such as from the puppies' nails), a blocked milk duct, weaning too early, or an infection. Call your vet immediately if you suspect your female Vizsla has mastitis, as puppies should not be allowed to nurse from mothers with this condition.

Newborn Puppy Health Problems

Below is a list of things you should check to identify whether your new litter is normal and healthy:

- Healthy suck reflex
- Normal and functioning urethra and anus
- No cleft palate
- Pink and moist gums and mucous membranes
- Healthy coat

Consider purchasing a baby scale to monitor the puppies' weight. They all should show gradual weight gain from birth to 12, 24, and 48 hours, to three, five, and seven days.

Young puppies are prone to diseases and infection, and a low body temperature puts stress on their already susceptible immune system. It also affects their ability to nurse and digest food, which gives their young bodies further stress. If a puppy becomes chilled, it is important to warm it slowly and to prevent it from feeding until it is back to its warm and stable temperature.

Keep your newborn puppies away from unvaccinated dogs and talk to your vet about parasite control.

The Vizsla Mom and Her Puppies

Keep the whelping box dry, clean, and warm. There may be some drainage and waste in the area for the next couple of weeks, so change the beddings daily. Cleanliness is key to maintaining a healthy environment for both the puppies and the mother.

Having their mom around is vital for the puppies' survival. Feeding will normally take place every two to three hours. They are unable to eat solid food until they are at least four weeks old. They should not be separated from the mother under any circumstances during this critical period. The mother should be given time to rest with her puppies and should not be disturbed. When the puppies are more than a month old, a mixture of dry food and milk can be introduced, before shifting to solid food. If circumstances prevent the mother from being with her pups, contact a veterinarian for a suitable substitute for her milk.

Watch for Warning Signs of Sickness

You will need to observe the puppies a lot during their first few weeks since they are unable to do anything on their own.

Contact your vet right away if you notice abnormalities in their appearance or behavior. Some things to look out for include excessive crying, vomiting, diarrhea, rejection by the mother, or if the puppy is not nursing with everyone else.

Vizsla Mix Puppies

Wirehaired Vizsla Puppies

These puppies are the result of breeding the Smooth-Coated Vizsla, and the German Wirehaired Pointer. This brought about a hunting dog with the grace and agility of the Vizslas, and the endurance and hardiness of the Pointer. They are related to the (very rare) Longhaired Vizsla.

Although it has many similarities with the smooth-coated Vizsla, the Wirehaired Vizsla's most obvious difference is its 1 to 2-inch (2.5 to 5 centimeters) long dense, wiry coat, which is golden rust in color, to help them blend in with dried grasses and bushes in the field. They are lean, with a slightly elongated body, and long legs. They are strong and can cover much ground with a few strides.

Vizsla Lab Mix Puppies

The Vizsla Lab Mix can also be called 'Labrala,' Vizslador, or 'Lablas.' It is a product of breeding the Vizsla and the Labrador retriever. These dogs both have high energy levels, and are affectionate, smart, and willing to please. They are also gentle-mannered and sensitive. It isn't a guarantee that their offspring will display these exact characteristics, but will most likely show similar traits.

Vizsla Lab Mix Health

All dogs have the potential to develop genetic health problems. A breeder should be able to guarantee the health of the puppy. The breeder should be open and honest about the health problems of their dogs. Health clearances prove that a dog has been tested for and cleared of a particular condition.

The Vizsla and the Chocolate Labrador mix might be prone to hip and elbow dysplasia, allergies, ear infections, eye problems, and bloat. These are common problems in both dog breeds.

Vizsla Lab Mix Care

Grooming Requirements

The Vizsla sheds less than the Labrador Retriever. You can bathe your Vizslador when necessary; too much will dry out their skin.

Exercise

Make it a habit of taking them for walks outside daily. If you don't find time to engage with them outside, they will probably turn your house into a playground!

Training Requirements

The Vizsla and Labrador Retriever are breeds that are easy to train, due to their high intelligence. You will need to complement their training with exercise to make it effective.

Vizsla Lab Mix Feeding

This mixed breed is prone to hip and elbow dysplasia, and as such, will do well with a diet that includes fish oil, glucosamine, and chondroitin supplements. Overfeeding for any dog is a bad idea and can only further health problems.

CHAPTER 11

Vizsla Breed Mixes

Different Types of Vizsla:

Wirehaired Vizsla

The Wirehaired Vizsla started to emerge in the 1930s. It was noticed at the time, that there were some Vizslas that had thicker coats. This protected the Vizsla better from extreme temperatures. One female Vizsla with the thicker coat was bred with a German Wirehaired Pointer. Mr. Vasas Josef was the first breeder who crossed the two breeds. He attempted to mate the same German Wirehaired Pointer with the different females. As a result, the Wirehaired Vizsla now has two cousins: the smooth-coated Vizsla and the Longhaired Vizsla.

The American Kennel Club officially recognized the Wirehaired Vizsla recently, in 2014.

Longhaired Vizsla

The Longhaired Vizsla is not an officially recognized breed, but more of a rare variation.

Hungarian Wirehaired Vizsla

Hungarian Vizslas and Hungarian Wirehaired Vizslas are seen as separate breeds. The latter is slightly bigger and stronger than the purebred Vizsla. Unlike the purebred Vizsla, the Hungarian Wirehaired Vizsla has a protective wire coat that can shield it from cold temperatures or rough cover.

The Hungarian Wirehaired Vizsla has a scruffy face, and the fur on its muzzle resembles a mustache. Their fur is golden rust in color. This breed is mostly seen outside of the US and takes on working roles.

Different Vizsla Coats

Grey Vizsla

If you see a Vizsla with a grey coat, it is probably a descendant of the Weimaraner, as one of the parent dogs, and a purebred Vizsla.

Black Vizsla

It is very rare to see a Vizsla with a black coat. It could be possible that one of its ancestors is a black Labrador mix.

Vizsla Breed Mixes

Vizsla Weimaraner Mix

This is a cross between a Vizsla and a Weimaraner. Both are excellent hunting breeds and are equally intelligent and energetic. This is a healthy mixed breed that can live up to 15 years.

The Vizsla and the Labrador Retriever share many characteristics, making them a good blend for the family.

Vizsla German Shepherd Mix

German Shepherds can be a good breed to cross with Vizslas. The German Shepherds are known for their excellent sense of smell, and this sense is very developed, compared to most dog breeds. Vizslas and German Shepherds are equally versatile and have high intelligence. Both are also loyal and ready to protect their family.

Vizsla Pitbull mix

Vizslas and Pitbulls share some characteristics that can complement one another. They are easy to maintain, thanks to their short coats that do not shed too much. The Pitbull can adapt more easily than the Vizsla. Both breeds demand plenty of exercise, so you need to be sure you can provide it if you aim to have this mixed breed.

Vizsla – Chocolate/Black/Yellow Lab Mix

The Vizsla and the Labrador Retriever share many characteristics, making them a good blend both for the family and as an outdoor companion. Both breeds are eager to please, friendly with both people and animals, and are easy to train. With their working and retrieving history, they are active dogs. These are the kind of dogs for which exercise is essential. Both breeds need physical and mental activities to keep them happy.

Before considering having these two dogs breed, get to know more about the Labrador, too!

Labradors are known to be a very good dog breed. However, Labs are large, high-energy animals that need to be trained. They love to eat, and this extends to people food, and even to inedible items! Allow them plenty of time for exercise. Being the working breed that they are, they have to be given an hour of exercise every day. Without it, just like the Vizsla, they might vent their energy onto your furnishings. Provide toys to channel their chewing habits, and to prevent them from getting bored.

The Lab ranks as America's number one dog, which means a lot of people could be breeding Labs who are only interested in meeting the demand for puppies, overlooking producing healthy dogs with good temperaments.

Looking for a Healthy Lab

If you want a healthy dog, avoid looking for it in pet stores, puppy mills, and breeders which make you question their motivations. Be patient when scrutinizing different breeders, to ensure your

Labrador is free from genetic diseases that might be passed on to the puppies. Make sure that the breeder can show the health clearances of their dogs and puppies.

Health

Like all other breeds, Labrador Retrievers are also prone to certain health conditions. Not all of them will contract any or all of these diseases, but it is also important to be aware of these if you are thinking of owning this breed. These diseases include:

- Hip and Elbow Dysplasia
- Osteochondrosis Dissecans (OCD)
- Cataracts
- Progressive Retinal Atrophy (PRA)
- Epilepsy
- Tricuspid Valve Dysplasia (TVD)
- Myopathy
- Gastric Dilatation-Volvulus (bloat)
- Acute Moist Dermatitis
- Cold Tail
- Ear Infections

Feeding

The recommended daily amount of food for a Labrador is 2.5 to 3 cups of high-quality dry food a day, divided into two meals.

Keep your Labrador fit and healthy by measuring its food, and feeding it twice a day rather than leaving food out all the time.

Keep track of a puppy Labrador's growth, as it can be very rapid between the age of four and seven months, making them susceptible to bone disorders.

Coat Color and Grooming

The Labrador coat comes in three colors: chocolate, black, and yellow. Black was the favorite color of early breeders, but over the years, chocolate and yellow Labradors have become popular. Recently, some breeders begun selling "rare" colored Labrador Retrievers - polar white or fox red. These shades aren't rare — they're a variation of the yellow Labrador. The coat has two layers: a short, thick, straight topcoat, and a soft, weather-resistant undercoat. Its coat protects it from cold temperatures and wet environments. These qualities make it an efficient retriever. Unlike the Vizsla, the Labrador sheds a lot. Bathe Labradors every two months to keep them clean and looking good.

Vizsla Golden Retriever Mix

Vizslas and Golden Retrievers are known to be great hunting companions. Crossing these breeds may amplify and improve their tracking and retrieving performance. Both breeds are also very active and energetic, so they need to have daily exercise and be allowed to run and stretch their legs. There may be a difference in temperament as Vizslas will be content to sit close to their owners, while the Golden Retriever is always looking forward to moving and playing with its family.

CHAPTER 12

Conclusion

The Vizsla, also known as the "Velcro" dog, is highly energetic and loyal. Originally from Hungary, it was bred for hunting and thrives best given a human companion. The Vizsla is eager to please, which makes them trainable. They also love to socialize, so make sure they are always invited to family activities!

Hunting is in a Vizsla's DNA, making them love the outdoors.

Hunting is in the Vizsla's DNA, so you need to give your dog the chance to perform this skill by letting it go out to the field. You can simulate this with toys in the park, as well. If you want things to be spic and span in the house, make it a part of your everyday routine to take your Vizsla out for exercise and play. It's that important. Having a fenced yard is a big help for both you and your Vizsla.

Owning the Vizsla is a huge commitment and responsibility that requires your time, effort, and energy to make sure your dog is nurtured.

Having a Vizsla as your companion will be a great experience full of exciting adventures and a fulfilling journey. Good luck and enjoy the ride!

BONUS CHAPTER

List of Additional Vizsla Resources

This resource list will help you learn even more about the Vizsla breed, Enjoy!

- **American Kennel Club**
  http://www.akc.org/dog-breeds/vizsla/care/
- **Au Sable Vizslas**
  http://www.ausablevizslas.com
- **Hungarian Vizsla Society**
  https://www.vizsla.org.uk
- **Hungarian Vizsla: The Ultimate Vizsla Guide**
  http://hungarian-vizsla.com
- **Hungarian Wirehaired Vizsla Association**
  http://hwva.org.uk/
- **It's A Vizsla Thing**
  http://vizslathing.blogspot.com
- **Rainbow Hungarian Vizsla Club**
  https://vizslaclub.co.za/
- **The Vizsla Club of America**
  http://www.vcaweb.org
- **Vizsla Central**
  http://vizslacentral.com

- **Vizsla Forums**
  http://www.vizslaforums.com/
- **Vizsla Club of Long Island**
  http://www.vcli.net
- **Wirehaired Vizsla Club of America**
  http://www.whvca.org
- **The Vizsla Club of America, Inc.**
  http://www.vcaweb.org/
- **Vizsla Canada Inc.**
  http://vizslacanada.ca
- **The Hungarian Vizsla Club UK**
  http://www.hungarianvizslaclub.org.uk

Printed in Great Britain
by Amazon

72861028R00078